EASTBOUND ECUMENISM

A Collection of Essays
on the World Council
of Churches and
Eastern Europe

Hans Hebly

UNIVERSITY
PRESS OF
AMERICA

LANHAM • NEW YORK

Free University Press
Amsterdam 1986

Copyright © 1986 by

Univeristy Press of America, ® Inc.

4720 Boston Way
Lanham, MD 20706

Printed in the United States of America

Co-published by arrangement with the
Interuniversity Institute for Missiological
and Ecumenical Research

Jointly published and distributed in Europe by
Free University Press

Free University Press is an imprint of
VU Boekhandel / Uitgeverij b.v.
De Boelelaan 1105
1081 HV Amsterdam
The Netherlands

Library of Congress Cataloging in Publication Data

Hebly, J. A.
    Eastbound ecumenism.

    Includes index.
    1. World Council of Churches—History.   2. Ecumenical
movement—History.   3. Europe, Eastern—Church history.
I. Title.
BR738.6.H39   1986   270.8'2   86-9137
ISBN 0-8191-5400-8 (alk. paper)
ISBN 0-8191-5401-6 (pbk. : alk. paper)

All University Press of America books are produced on acid-free
paper which exceeds the minimum standards set by the National
Historical Publications and Records Commission.

to Peter

Table of contents

page

PREFACE

The situation of the churches in Eastern Europe is highly diversified, but the impact of their limited possibilities -some of them find themselves in a political and ideological captivity- on their ecumenical activities needs to be more critically studied than has been done up till now.

Hence the appeal in this book to take the relationship with these churches, living in a society determined by Marxism-Leninism, more seriously. Not the mere relationship itself, but its form and content ought to be critically evaluated.

A profound change has taken place since a Western shaped Christian universalism led to the formation of the World Council of Churches.

This can no longer be taken for granted. In fact, such premisses are no longer generally accepted; and the fact that the churches now have to fulfill their mission in completely different and mutually opposed social systems profoundly affects their collaboration in the social and political field: a fact which especially spokesmen of the Evangelical Churches in the GDR seem to take into account. The problem of East-West ecumenical relations, which has so strongly affected the European ecumene, has given way to other priorities in the World Council of Churches: such as Third World issues. But the various social and political problems in our divided world are closely related to each other: therefore East-West problems must not be neglected.

It seems a hazardous enterprise to raise the question: Can the World Council of Churches continue to function as a common body for witness and service of churches from East and West in the way which has been followed in the last twenty years? Time and time again, voices have been heard which complain about the selectivity of the causes for which the World Council of Churches really engages itself, about the fact that the issue of religious liberty threatens to disappear from its agenda, about the fact that its prophetic witness hardly seems to direct itself to the world of 'really-existing socialism'. Is there real cause for such criticism; and, if so, which alternative ways could be indicated? Although no clear-cut scheme has been developed to show how, in the present world, the universality of the Church of Christ can be realised in its social and political witness, the non-prejudiced reader will find a number of constructive ideas, which could be helpful to overcome the present crisis.

Part of Chapter I has been published in Ökumenische Rundschau (Jhrg. 28, 1979, S. 421-439). Chapter III has already appeared in Occasional Papers on Religion in Eastern Europe (Vol. 4, 1984-3) and Chapter V. in Religion in Communist Lands (Vol. 13, 1985-2).

J.A. (Hans) Hebly

Chapter I

THE REGIONALISATION OF THE ECUMENICAL MOVEMENT: A VIABLE WAY?

What is happening now to the ecumenical movement and its official forum: i.e. the World Council of Churches? "Something young and vigorous, something endued with hope and vision, something which is the focus of prayers and aspirations of many millions", as Sir Kenneth Grubb once put it, seems to have become unsure about its present tasks in a world more divided than ever.

The growth of the ecumenical movement in the protestant world really started in 1895 in Vadstena in Sweden with the foundation of the World Student Christian Federation. It was the period of the expansion of the Western world. The universalistic tendency in Western culture influenced leading circles in the churches and is at the basis of the movements which led to the formation of the WCC. The ecumenical movement first began to take shape not on the level of the local and regional churches, but in the form of international movements. A world council came into existence before local and regional councils had been established. Ecumenical bodies have always stressed the necessity that the ecumenical ideal must also establish itself at the grass-roots. But, when it did, some serious questionmarks began to be put against some important aspects of the World Council itself. Was it not an expression of the dominant Western culture? And is it not breaking up into a plurality of Christian communities adapted to controversial political systems?

In New Delhi, in 1961, the main accent in the famous definition of unity was put on unity in the local church. A new chapter could begin. 1961 seems to mark the end of a development and the beginning of a new period. The WCC had, by then, reached a certain fullness. The International Missionary Council and the Eastern Churches joined the universal fellowship. What the pioneers from 1895 onwards had wanted and strived for was attained, or almost attained; because the Roman Catholic Church still remained outside this universal Christian fellowship. The summit of the Alps was reached; but then they saw, not the pleasant green pastures of steady and quiet development, but a new landscape with still more difficult peaks to climb.

The rise of the ecumenical movement at the high-tide of the new Western imperialism

Ecumenical historiography has long been characterized by its optimistic even triumphalistic tone. The 'great new fact of our era'(1) was being described in a sphere of optimism and progress. The word 'advance' played a prominent role. H.E. Fey called his second volume of the history of the ecumenical movement 'The

Ecumenical Advance'. K.C. Latourette entitled his book about the expansion of Christianity (Vol. VII) 'Advance through Storm'. The new ecumenism, awakening in the protestant world, was being regarded as the unfolding of an inherent but neglected part of protestant ecclesiology: the universality and catholicity of the church. Mission, service, unity and renewal determined the various streams which finally came together in the World Council of Churches. Geographical names marked the road of development: Edinburgh, Stockholm, Lausanne, Jerusalem, Madras, Amsterdam, Evanston, New Delhi and so forth... For theologians, these names indicate a profound theological development, different phases in a process of growth. They are the bench-marks of the progress of the church towards unity and universality.

But it is a remarkable fact that very little attention has been given to an analysis of the cultural, social and other factors which also determined the rise of the ecumenical movement. The famous 'History of the Ecumenical Movement 1517-1948' by R. Rouse and S.C. Neill does not pose the question of why the ecumenical idea began to play a role in the life of the churches only in the first half of the 20th century and one will hardly find any mention of the creation of the many international organisations which have their origins in the second half of the 19th century. The formation of a large number of international organisations preceded the formation of the WCC.

> World Exhibitions starting with the Crystal Palace Exhibition (1851), Red Cross (1864), Lambeth Conference (1867), World Alliance of Reformed Churches (1875), Salvation Army (1880), Ecumenical Methodist Conference (1881), World Sunday School Convention (1889), World Parliaments of Religions (1893), Olympic Games (1896), the Scouting Movement (1897), The International Association for Labour Legislation (1900; 1919 International Labour Organisation), the World Congress of Liberal Christianity (1900), the philanthropic work of the Rockefeller Foundation (1901), officially recognized in 1913 as an institution 'to promote the well-being of mankind throughout the world'.

The roots of the ecumenical movement and the blossoming of a new universalism in the protestant world are to be found in the high-tide of western expansion, at a time when almost all the international organisations which we know at present had their origin. "At first the ecumenical movement was especially in its Life and Work branche a wave in the general democratic-idealistic spring-tide", writes Berkhof (2). And an IDOC paper (3) speaks about the theological and sociological presuppositions, which were at the basis of the ecumenical movement and which do not exist any longer. H.P. van Dusen (4) calls the ecumenical pioneers children of the (19th) century, characterized by a strong world-consciousness, the idea of expansion and a calling towards the whole of mankind.

The pioneers of the ecumenical movement had their spiritual roots in the period from 1890 to 1914: a time of unprecedented expansion of the Western world and of 'the emerging world culture'(5) which had its origin in the Occident. By 1900, 'European civilization overshadowed the earth'(6). "From the heart of the new industrial societies forces went out which encompassed and transformed the whole world." In 1876 no more than one-tenth of Africa was controlled by European powers, by 1900 nine-tenths of the continent was under European control(7).

The high-tide of the new imperialism was caused, among other things, by the rising number of the European population and the new industrial and economic developments. It is not necessary to invoke a Marxist view of history to see at least a parallel between Western expansion and Christian mission in these days.
Mission was mainly an Anglo-Saxon enterprise. Seven-eighths of the mission field was evangelized by Anglo-Saxons. "When merchants were dreaming in terms of new markets, when statesmen were planning fresh colonial adventures, it was natural for the more earnest among the Christians to seek to parallel these movements with others for the world-wide extension of their faith."
"Expansion, pioneering and adventure were in the air." There was a general "air of hope and expansion which permeated much of the Occident, notably Great-Britain and the United States" - a rapid growth of commerce and an improvement of communications, but also a "burst of new life within Christianity itself"(8).
This new life expressed itself in pietistic revival movements which were very influential at colleges and in the universities: e.g. L. Moody (1837-1899) and Henry Drummond, 'the most powerful student evangelist yet seen'(9). A combination of individualism, a stress on the creative liberty of the individual, which also showed itself in commerce and industry, with an optimistic trust in progress and the unlimited possibilities for the future, marked the spiritual climate. The Christians were children of their time and participated in the movements which characterized that period.

In student-circles, there was great interest in missions. The Student Volunteer Movement for Foreign Mission started in 1886. John Mott was its president from 1888 until 1920. No less than 18.000 volunteers went out into the mission fields under the auspices of this organisation before 1924. In a report -The first two decades of the Student Volunteer Movement(10) - it is said: "It is no mere coincidence that in the very generation which has seen the whole world made open and accessible and the nations and races drawn so closely together by the influence of commerce there has been created this world-wide student brotherhood." J. Verkuyl(11), a Dutch missiologist, calls the Student Volunteer Movement "the greatest missionary movement since Whitsun". Behind the mission stood the rich commercial and industrial Western élite, typified for instance by John Rockefeller who was called 'the most important financier of liberal and ecumenical protestantism'(12). The YMCA-centres all over the world are a clear sign of their generosity. Western power and influence spread over the world and a new universalism emerged with the spread all over the world of Western goods, ideas and values - a pax atlantica.

The universalistic tendencies in the gospel were discovered anew in this cultural climate by the potestants. Because Jesus Christ died for all, all must hear the Gospel. What was latent came to the fore -new creative impulses, which influenced those who became pioneers of the ecumenical movement- a cultural élite. But it remained confined to a group of outstanding men and women. Did this new universalism, of which the WCC is a late fruit, not remain on the outside of church and theology?

Has this rediscovering of the universality and catholicity of the church given rise to a renewal in the life and thinking of the churches or rather was its influence restricted to a relatively small group of a world-open élite?
The Ecumenical Movement was in those first years formed by a circle of friends. The ecumenical pioneers had their origins in the World Student Christian Federation. A biographer of John Mott, a leader in the World Student Christian Federation from 1895 until his death, wrote(13): 'As Mott looked into the faces of the delegates at Lausanne and picked out those who in the early days of the WSCF had come into that movement, he had a joyful realisation of the gift of the student movement to ecumenical Christianity on all continents'. And Oxford (1937) was according to Van Dusen 'a reunion of old schoolboys'.(14)

From Vadstena to New Delhi

    The foundation of the WSCF in a medieval castle in Vadstena, Sweden, 1895, is really the birth-hour of the modern ecumenical movement and there is a direct line from the student movement in the second half of the 19th century to the WCC.
The Student Volunteers formed a creative group, a real élite, a sort of new protestant order, compared by Sherwood Eddy to the creation of the Jesuit order. One had the impression, wrote Eddy(15), that a new chapter was being added to the Acts of the Apostles. We may add that the WSCF, as a driving force in the world ecumene, has since died: it has now been reduced in many places to a small group linked with the Christians for Socialism.

4

That optimistic nineteenth century belief in progress had a moving effect in the Western protestant world. Exceptional and eminent personalities came to the fore and the world was their parish. Children of their time, usually from upper middle-class circles, well-educated, liberal, individualists, who worked for individual conversions and wanted, if not to build the Kingdom of God, then at least to prepare for its coming. They were the exponents of the best that the Western world had to offer and contributed much to the formation of the 'westernized oriental gentlemen'(16) who soon started to play their part in the Ecumenical Movement.

It was this group, inspired by John Mott, which injected the missions with their ecumenical idea. They wanted to unite the separate protestant forces and were, rather than the missionary boards at home, at the base of the ecumenical inspiration of the missions and the younger churches.

"Under the influence of these united Volunteers, in common with other causes at work, the idea of Christian unity has been more fully realized on the mission field than at home."(17).

The most typical representative of that time, who can without any doubt be called the father of the WCC, was John Mott. This American gentleman, closely related to all those who shaped the Western expansion, was a typical representative of the spiritual dimension of his age.

One of his adresses after 1910, with which he travelled round the world, was entitled 'Christianizing the impact of Western civilization'(18). A Western concept of the universality of the Church prevailed: "The church can be the common bond and the moral and spiritual basis of the world-culture."(19). And one of Mott's famous statements was 'see the world as a whole, a unit and the church as a unit."(20). But it was a unity of the world under Western political and spiritual dominance. The question of unity was answered from a North-Atlantic perspective. Unity was a fruit of Western culture, seen as the dominating world culture and the creation of the WCC could, in this perspective, be regarded as a late fruit of an interesting but now definitely closed chapter of the history of the Western world.

Did the re-discovery of the universality and catholicity of the Church in those days really take its rise in the deep sources of the faith of the protestant churches? And has it really fundamentally influenced those churches? Or has it been a temporary cultural influence on the churches which in another historical period are now sliding back into provincialism?

In a time in which almost all of the present international organisations have their origin, the WCC came into existence. At that moment, sociological and cultural presuppositions led to the formation of the WCC. The idea was 'in the air' as Visser 't

Hooft wrote in the History of the Ecumenical Movement(21). But it could well be that in our days we must look for other forms. Sociological, cultural and theological preconditions are now quite different. Most probably we must travel along a much longer and much more difficult way before the seed -the universality and the catholicity of the Church- will really become fruitful.

"The world as a unit and the Church as a unit" seemed to have been attained: but new developments have wakened us up from this dream. The growth of the ecumenical movement must be seen against the background of the expansion of the Western world. The universalism which influenced leading circles in the protestant churches was strongly influenced by cultural factors. It has taken a long time before theology began to think about the christological character of the new universalism. Visser 't Hooft remarked that only the Faith and Order movement began to see Christ as the centre of Christian universalism. In his book 'No other name' he speaks about the Christian universalism which he sees rooted in the Gospel and he regards the ecumenical movement as an attempt to realize this specific Christian universalism. He describes the contribution of the Missionary Society, Faith and Order and Life and Work who fused together in 1961. But the history of the Ecumenical Movement is restricted here to the development of a number of international organisations and the influence of this Christian universalism on the life of the local churches is not really fathomed.

This influence should not be overestimated. Christian universalism has not really touched upon the life and structures of the churches and the thinking of the faithful. It is interesting to note that from 1961 onwards -the New Delhi conference- we see a shift of perspective. The search for the wholeness of the Church which started with the creation of international organisations and which was pursued in world-perspective, should be realised on the local level and from there extend to a wider circle of the communion of all: not the other way round(22).

Towards a regionalised ecumenical movement

The British historian, Geoffrey Barraclough, writes that between 1955 and 1960 the world moved into a new historical period with different dimensions and different problems of its own; and this is reflected in the Ecumenical Movement. The universalism which was so strongly marked by the preceding period, came into a real crisis. The period of decolonization and resistance to Atlantic domination strongly began to influence the world-ecumene. There is now, in our world, a clearly-defined process of political regionalisation: e.g. the organisations of African, Latin-American, Asiatic and Arabic countries which arose after the Bandung Conference of Asiatic and African countries in

1955. The block of socialist countries began to play a really dominant role in international life after the death of Stalin in 1953. The United Nations are passing through a very critical period because of the formation of regional blocks and the predominant position of the Western world is constantly questioned. Parallel to the political regionalisation, we notice a tendency to regionalisation in the Ecumenical Movement, beginning with the East Asian Christian Conference in 1959. Weber says in the Ecumenical Advance(23) that ecumenical regionalisation has nothing to do with the formation of continental or racial power blocks. But should we not be more modest and more realistic and see the ecumenical regionalisation as a parallel to the phenomenon of political regionalisation? Lukas Vischer(24) asks whether the churches can still pretend to play an independent role on the world scene. Should they not confine themselves to exercise a critical function in the different ideological and political systems? A quite different concept of the role of the Church from that of John Mott, who saw the Church as the common bond and the moral and spiritual basis of the world culture. But a Westernized form of universalism now belongs to a past period of history. The Universal Declaration of Human Rights adopted by the United Nations in 1948 is now criticised, for instance, by the socialist and the Third World countries as a product of a Western, liberal, humanistic culture, which saw itself as universal and thought it possible to impress its norms and values upon the whole world.

There is also a cultural regionalisation. H. Kraemer wrote in his book 'Religion and Culture' that, in the confrontation with the West, a stronger consciousness of their own cultural identities has arisen in other regions of the world. Nowadays, we hear much criticism of the oppressive structures of Western theology, a protest against the universal pretensions of Western theological thinking: and we see at the same time a sort of regionalisation of theological experience and thinking wich is called contextualization. In the theological thinking in the ecumene there have been important developments since the beginning of the sixties. H. Berkhof said in his Berkelbachlectures(25):

"After the lecture of E. Käsemann in Montreal 1963 -Unity and Plurality in the N.T. Teaching about the Church- I met a very depressed and unhappy Visser 't Hooft who said: it is dreadful, a man like Käsemann is destroying my life-work. Then I answered: No, that is not true, the unity as we have seen it up till now does exist, but in this form it was a prematurely won victory. The speech of Käsemann meant that from that moment onwards the pluriformity and plurality in the Church were much more accentuated."

Here, the basis was prepared for a more regionalised theological development. Cultural and sociological factors influence theological thinking: that much is clear already. The world entered a new period and theology followed suit. After 1960 we can also notice another very important development. The Roman Catholic Church became more and more involved in the Ecumenical Movement. In comparison with the Protestant Churches, the Roman Catholic Church is a universal church: and we see that after 1962 a new theological discussion arises of which Rome is the centre. A series of bilateral conversations have taken place in which the churches are now asking the Roman Catholic Church how far it will develop towards a truly evangelical Catholic Church. This is still going on; but what is noteworthy in this respect is that the Roman Catholic Church will not apparently join the WCC, but puts the main accent on ecumenical collaboration on the local and regional level. The ecumenical Directorium of 1975 opens up many new possibilities in this respect.

The Russians on the side-lines

One of the most interesting and challenging new developments in the sixties was the arrival of the Russian Orthodox Church on the world ecumenical scene. A number of Orthodox Churches from the socialist world followed suit. The New Delhi Assembly (1961) greeted with joy and satisfaction the entry of a church which, up till then, had remained consistently aloof from the world-ecumene. The Secretary of the Vatican Secretariat for the Promotion of Christian Unity, called it in a letter to W.A. Visser 't Hooft(26) 'a fact of historical importance.'

"I do not doubt the Christian motives which on both sides have led to this step. Nevertheless this fact is at the same time a critical moment in the development of the World Council of Churches and this will appear probably more clearly in the future."

These words would prove to be prophetic. Although the membership of the Council received a more universal dimension, the Western shape of ecumenical universalism was severely dented.
The entry of the Russian Orthodox Church into the World Council of Churches was only one aspect of its new and rather surprising overture to the world-ecumene.

In the same year, 1961, the Pan-Orthodox conferences started with a meeting in Rhodos to prepare for a Great and Holy Pan-Orthodox Synod. The aim of the conference was to study ways of bringing closer together and uniting the churches in a Pan-Orthodox perspective. These conferences have been continued since and the Russian Church plays a predominant role in them. In 1962, the

Russian Orthodox Church decided rather unexpectedly to send observers to the Second Vatican Council.

These steps were preceded by the involvement of the Russian Church in two regional ecumenical organisations. In 1959 the Conference of European Churches was founded in Nyborg, Denmark, and the Russians were founding-members. And, in June 1958, in Prague, a first meeting took place of the Christian Peace Conference: an ecumenical body in which the churches from Eastern Europe combined their activities in the field of peace-work. Albert Boiter called this meeting 'a watershed event'(27).

"The June 1958 meeting in Prague was a watershed event in the sense that religious leaders from different confessions in Eastern Europe were permitted to meet openly for any purpose at all and that this opened the door to a proliferation of international contacts of many kinds between religious leaders of East and West in the 1960s, whereas such contacts were almost nonexistent before the late 1950s.
It was a watershed also because it signified an important change of attitude by communist leaders, especially the Soviet Communist Party headed by Khrushchev, about the possible utility of trustworthy church leaders appearing as concrete examples of the newly-emerging policy of peaceful coexistence, which in 1958 still meant essentially the desire of the Soviet Union to break out of its Stalin-era isolation onto the world political stage. In any event, the first CPC gathering in Prague did not take place without the prior knowledge and approval of Moscow, although the exact form and content of that approval is not a matter of public record. Moscow chose a rather oblique means of bestowing its nihil obstat on Dr. Hromadka's 'experiment': it awarded him the Lenin Peace Prize for his services to the cause of communism at home and abroad, especially in the world ecumenical movement. The text of the award was published in Pravda on May 30, 1958, one day before the Prague conference opened."

The Christian Peace Conference can be regarded as the beginning of a regional ecumenical organisation, which has, however, since the seventies tried to direct its attention, mainly for political motives, on contacts with the Third World. Probably because of that, regional consultations have been organised by the churches in the socialist countries to combine their ecumenical efforts since 1974. Churches have a way of following political trends and the churches in Eastern Europe are not different in this respect.

The years around 1960, strangely enough one of the most difficult periods in the recent history of the Russian Church, marked by internal persecution and restrictions, saw a blossoming of ecumenical activities and the opening of a new chapter in its external relations.

During the formative years of the modern ecumenical movement, the Russian Orthodox Church stood on the side-lines. It was not actively engaged in any of the movements which contributed to the formation of the World Council of Churches.
A very interesting series of articles appeared in The Journal of the Moscow Patriarchate(28) on the subject of 'The Ecumenical Movement and the Russian Orthodox Church before she joined the World Council of Churches'. The authors clearly show that the questions of Christian unity and the attitudes to non-Christians were heatedly debated in the Russian Orthodox Church from the 19th century onwards. Contacts were established with Old-Catholics and Anglicans and the Bonn Reunion Conferences; but, apart from these theological dialogues, a relationship with ecumenical circles in the West did not develop. The remark of Patriarch Pimen(29) about 'the original, not only purely Western, but entirely pro-Western character of the structure, activity and politico-social orientation of the World Council of Churches' does not only apply to the period of its establisment. For the Russian Church it has always been a Western movement. John Mott visited Russia during his many travels in 1899 and 1909. He spoke at students meetings and small interconfessional circles were set up in some university centres, which were included in the World Student Christian Federation by 1913 and continued for a brief interlude before war and revolution destroyed them. But after the 1909 visit the Holy Synod decreed that Mott should never be allowed to return to Russia(30). He did return, however, as member of a special mission of the US government to the Provisional Government of Russia, which arrived in Petrograd on June 15, 1917. He was then received at the Holy Synod and even invited to adress the Synod: 'an honor, rarely, if ever before accorded to a Protestant'.
"I congratulated them on the future, showing them why the best days of the Russian church lie in the years before us."

Those were tragic days for the Russians; but, at the same time, full of expectations of a better future, apparently shared by this American visitor. Who could have expected that the most disastrous period for Russian believers was about to begin?
No 'advance through storm', but a time of martyrdom: the most severe ordeal through which any church in history has ever to pass. It would take another World War before the church in the Soviet Union could establish contact with sister-churches in the rest of the world and after a thirty years period of isolation seek to join the ecumenical movement. It is perhaps one of the most tragic aspects of the present situation that the Russian Orthodox Church, now a powerful member of the world-ecumene, is forced to keep silent about this time of suffering. The spiritual

wealth and the deep experience which this church has accumulated cannot be brought into the ecumenical fellowship to enrich and deepen its spirituality. The Journal writes, for instance, about this periode only as 'going through a difficult period of formation in new socio-political conditions and intra-church schism'. But its isolation from ecumenical developments before 1961 was also caused by its being a statechurch closely linked with the official administration and, even before the revolution, supervised and dominated by the state administration. The orthodox theologian J. Zizioulas remarked(32) that the autocephalic structure of the Orthodox churches has prevented these churches from becoming an instrument of cultural expansion and domination. But, in reality, the Russian Orthodox Church has, probably because of its autocephaly, become a classic example of a church which has been used as a vehicle of nationalism and cultural domination. Russia has not incorrectly been called(33) 'the most compact colonial empire': and Orthodoxy functioned as its national ideology. Its expansion was closely linked with the expansion of the empire. The parallel which we have seen between Western imperialism and Christian mission can also be found in Orthodoxy. Religio and Imperium have always been intimately connected.

So it was in the times that the pax occidentalis was imposed on what we have become used to call the Third World. And so it was too in the vast Russian empire. And thus, to a certain extent, it still is in the Soviet Union. One of the recent tragic examples of cultural political domination has been the elimination of the Uniate churches in the Ukraine and their enforced integration into the Russian Orthodox Church after the Second World War.

The Russian Orthodox Church has joined the World Council of Churches; but, at the same time, it favours the regional organisations of churches in socialist countries. It has not shared the long process of ecumenical development through which the Western churches have passed and which has shaped their ecumenical ideals and attitudes. It entered the movement which it regarded as purely Western in order to find support for its threatened position; but also with a political commission to further Eastern policies and serve the cause of 'socialism'. It has not found the freedom to develop, independently of the state, its own ecumenical policy; but seems to be forced again to function as the vehicle of national aspirations and policies. The process of regionalisation of the ecumenical movement in the socialist countries seems to be strongly influenced by political factors. It is, indeed, a real danger and a constant temptation for the churches to allow themselves to be used for nationalistic and political ends.
To counterbalance this tendency, it will be necessary for the World Council of Churches to put before churches and governments

the necessity of the freedom and independence of the church. Only then can local, regional and universal ecumenical organisations function. I fully agree with Patriarch Pimen when he says(34)

"The experience we have, shows that there is no single, universal all-Christian answer possible here. The specific conditions and the lives of Christians in different circumstances, differences between cultures, economic and political systems, the variations between geographical regions and many other factors, which make the lives of Christians and churches so different and so unlike each other, all this means that there can and must be different answers to (our ecumenical study) themes, answers by faith in our Lord Jesus Christ as God and Saviour, Who liberates and unites us all, and Who is our ultimate hope and Whom we must confess in any of the conditions of our earthly existence."

Universal answers to the problems of our divided world are no longer possible; and this implies a change in ecumenical thinking. But a world council of churches should remain, if only as a constant witness to the liberty which any national or regional churchbody should have to be able to confess the name of Christ and fulfill its calling.

Conclusion

The process of regionalisation will go on: and, furthermore, the Central Committee of the WCC in 1976 was quite right to commend a study of the possibilities of regionalising the work of the WCC. Günther Gassmann(35) speaks of a challenge for the WCC which will have to function in future in a new and different way. He pleads for an intensification of the study-work and for a coordinating task of the WCC. It should function as a clearing-house, a place where dialogue between the confessions can take place; where evangelicals and progressives can meet; where an exchange can take place between theologians; and the dangers of a theological provincialism can be overcome through universal cross-fertilization. But many tasks could be delegated to regional ecumenical bodies.
The WCC is in many respects the late fruit of a bygone period, but that does not mean that it has now become useless. There is still the task to realize the wholeness of the Church, to stress its universality and catholicity. In the period which is behind us, the Ecumenical Movement has taken shape at the international level; but it has not really penetrated into the life and thinking of the local churches. The ecumenical ideals have mainly been confined to a restricted circle of a world-open elite.
The main accent is now being placed upon the local level and the regional ecumene. On that level, and in that context, we must now work for unity in worship, service and witness. But we should

take care not to fall back into provincialism. We should not step back from the vision of the Church Universal; but, rather, start at home and from there seek the communion of all. We might probably then be able to find new forms of a real Christian universalism: a universalism which is not just the by-product of an expanding and dominating Western culture, but the product of Christ's unifying work.

Church life and theology are bound up with the social situation and we see in our days the rise of contextual theologies engaged in the life and struggles of a country or a region. The unity of the church seems to be breaking up into a plurality of particular theological schools and of Christian communities adapted to controversial political systems or engaged in complicated situations with which other churches can hardly establish solidarity. This process cannot be stopped by wishful thinking, but has to be accepted. At the same time, however, these very diverse developments should be related to each other, cross-fertilize each other, stimulate and correct each other. In the dialectics of contextual regionalism and ecumenical universalism, a World Council has a specific role to play. It should in all modesty try to find possibly new ways to fulfill this very important function. But can an independent, autonomous form of Christian universalism be worked out by churches emphasizing the need for theological thinking which starts from the practice of a church living in a given historical and socio-political context? It seems that, at the present time, a difficult challenge is confronting the ecumenical movement. Christian universalism has become suspect in the eyes of peoples from the Third World as an expression of Western, atlantic dominance. Their struggle for independence and for finding their own course away from mother-countries does not stimulate a new vision of universalism. In the eyes of peoples from the Second World, churches in the capitalist part of the world are regarded as being in the service of the ruling classes of society and subjected to political misuse; and their universalism is suspected of being the spiritual expression of capitalist, neo-colonialist expansion. It is clear that, in the West, the suspicion is very much alive that the ecumenical initiatives originating from churches in the socialist countries are at the service of political forces which try to impress on the world their own socio-political concepts. These suspicions influence, and to a certain extent mark, the ecumenical attitudes of the churches. Christian universalism has arrived at a serious crisis: just like many other forms of international, world-wide organizations which were established in a bygone period of modern history.

What seems to be necessary at present is a strenuous effort to develop a real ecumenical theology. The Christian church is the bearer of a profound and creative universalism. This is not something added to the church by the cultural climate in which it lives, but belongs to the essence of its life and message. That will have to be made clear and worked out. The roots of real Christian universalism do not lie in secular concepts of unity. The churches are often giving good reasons for the suspicion, which still haunts the ecumenical movement, that secular concepts of unity and division dominate its work. The only way to overcome this is to find the roots of the universalism in the depositum fidei of the Church.

This may be clarified by an example from the discussion on religious liberty in the World Council of Churches. The great declarations of Amsterdam and New Delhi on this subject are presented even by spokesmen of the World Council itself as products of Western thinking and the Western way of life: individualistic, liberal, claiming the privileges of dominating churches. They are suspected of being founded on cultural rather than real Christian conceptions. But that which is brought forth against them is itself open to the suspicion of being marked by other culturalideological influences.
And so the ecumenical discussion at this point has almost come to a standstill. The only way out of this predicament is a new theological-anthropological study of the Christian basis of religious liberty. When the ecumene assumes that it will be impossible to come to a common expression of what the Christian faith has to say on religious liberty, this will mean the end of the Christian ecumene. It is self-evident that the realisation of social religious liberty will remain a problem in many parts of the world. But it should be made clear that the churches have a common mind and a common attitude on the basis of the fundamentals of their common faith. In this field of common study and discussion lies the main task for a council in which churches from all regions of the world are trying to cooperate.

The protestant churches are seeking to find new forms for the realization of the catholicity and universality of the church. In their ecclesiology this has generally been a forgotten chapter. The forms of their church-structures have been strongly marked by cultural-historical impulses, dominant in a certain historical period. This seems also to be true of the forms in which they try to express their universality. They have, especially since 1961, tried to find support in the Orthodox tradition. But Orthodoxy, with its leaning towards an identification with national-cultural and political entities, has not really been able to give new and stimulating impulses to the churches which arose during the reformation period.

But are we not on the threshold of a new period in ecumenical history? There is one catholic and universal church which has been able to express in its ecclesiology and life the universal dimension of the Christian church. The Roman Catholic Church may not according to many observers, have found the ultimate answers in the dialectical process of particularity and universality of the church. But the way in which it lives and experiences the tensions between regionalisation and universality could contain some very useful lessons for the protestant and the orthodox traditions. The present trend in the ecumenical movement towards regionalisation and the constant difficulty to find ways for an autonomous expression of the universal dimension of the Christian church in protestantism and orthodoxy might lead to a raprochement with the model offered by the Roman Catholic Church. For many, this might be a very questionable prospect: especially at the present moment when relations between Geneva and Rome seem to be at a low ebb. But, in essence, the problems and the challenges are identical: i.e. how to find the right balance between contextuality and universality, between the local, regional and the universal church. And above all: how to realize the unity of the Church of Christ in an autonomous way, free from the world but at the service of the world and of the brotherhood of all mankind.

NOTES

1. W. Temple at his enthronement in Canterbury 1942: F.A. Iremonger, William Temple, London 1948, p. 387.
2. Geschiedenis der Kerk, p. 297, 298
3. Crise de l'oecuménisme institutionel, IDOC International nr. 18-1970
4. Het Christendom in de Wereld, Amsterdam 1948, p. 60
5. K.S. Latourette, A History of the Expansion of Christianity IV, New York 1941, p. 21
6. G. Barraclough, An Introduction to contemporary history 1974, p. 61, 64.
7. D. Thompson, Europe since Napoleon, 12.1976, p. 498
8. Latourette o.c., p. 20, 76, 45
9. R. Rouse, The World Student Christian Federation 1948, p. 32
10. B. Mathews, John R. Mott, World Citizen, 1943, p. 223
11. Inleiding in de nieuwere zendingswetenschap, 1975, p. 248
12. P. Collier/D. Horowitz, The Rockefellers, 1976, p. 150
13. Mathews o.c., p. 245
14. o.c., p. 95
15. 80 Avontuurlijke jaren, p. 34
16. Barraclough o.c., p. 176
17. Mathews o.c., p. 225
18. ibidem, p. 217
19. Latourette VII, p. 27
20. Rouse o.c., p. 97
21. p. 698
22. o.c., p. 35
23. p. 70
24. Veränderung der Welt - Bekehrung der Kirchen, 1976, p. 68.
25. Publication Interuniversity Institute for Missiological and Ecumenical Research, Utrecht
26. J.A. Hebly, The Russians and the World Council of Churches, p. 117.
27. The Christian Peace Conference, 1958-1983. A political overview. Paper presented at the AAASS National Convention, Kansas City, 1983
28. 1983-11 till 1984-6
29. C.G. Parelos (ed.) The Orthodox Church in the Ecumenical Movement, 1978, p. 327
30. C. Howard Hopkins, John R. Mott 1865-1955, 1979, p. 335, 503
31. 1984-2, p. 63
32. Paper presented at a Consultation of the Conference of European Churches, Sofia, 1977
33. Barraclough o.c., p. 62, 86
34. Patelos o.c., p. 334
35. Die Regionalisierung der ökumenischen Bewegung, Zeichen der Zeit 10-74, p. 369-372.

Chapter II

THE POST-WAR ECUMENICAL DREAM IN EUROPE

It is quite possible that the ecumenical movement in Europe
will be regarded by future historians as a post-World War II
phenomenon, as an aspect of a period of reconstruction. The
prevailing mood in those days was one of renewal - society and
the church ought to find new ways after the apocalyptic disasters
which had left behind a trail of moral and material destruction.
The ecumenical idea, the influence of which had been confined to
part of the intellectual élite, achieved much wider scope and
seemed to offer just that perspective for which many good-willing
people were longing. The aim of the ecumenical movement had been
defined as the renewal of the Church to unity and to service. Not
just the reunion of the separated Christian communities: but,
rather, a new conception of the relation of the church to the
world and to society was implied in the ecumenical ideal. A whole
series of new problems confronted the churches and it was felt
not to be enough to secure the continued existence of the church.
What was required was to meet totally new demands on Christian
witness and service in a changing social and political scene. And
these tasks could only be accomplished by the churches together.
Outstanding church-leaders personified those ecumenical ideals:
W.A. Visser 't Hooft and H. Kraemer (Netherlands), M. Boegner and
Madeleine Barot (France), M. Niemöller and G. Heinemann
(Germany), G.K.A. Bell (Gt. Britain), E. Berggrav (Norway), and
many others, whose leadership had been tested in the dark days of
the war, became the spiritual mentors of a new generation of
European ecumenical theologians.

The reconstruction of a new Europe and the role which the
churches could play stood in the foreground of ecumenical activities. Ecumenism in Europe was experienced as a movement for
theological-biblical renewal with outspoken social implications.
Suzanne de Dietrich, one of the first staff-members of the Ecumenical Institute at 'Bossey', which was in the first period
especially intended to play a keyrole in the formation of
Christian lay-people who could be enabled to play a leading part
in the renewal of the life of the churches - an ecumenical
'Evangelische Akademie' - published her books on Le dessein de
Dieu and Le renouveau biblique.
The French ecumenical organisation Cimade for evangelisation,
social reconstruction and aid to refugees and displaced persons,
which had played a remarkable role during the war -Les Clandestins de Dieu-(1) was immensely popular in European ecumenical
circles and at the Amsterdam Assembly of the World Council of
Churches (1948). An immense relief-programme in warstricken

17

Europe was pushed through by the churches. For many Europeans, the ecumene was associated in those days and long afterwards with the humanitarian aid, received through the churches, in which they experienced the reality of the life of the church; and which opened their eyes for the church as a universal fellowship. Robert C. Mackie, Director of the Department of Inter Church Aid and Service to Refugees in Geneva wrote in 1951(2):

"Inter-Church Aid has been a distinctive factor in binding the Churches of Europe together... Today the churches must be ready to meet new situations created by explusions of people from one country to another, or by the disastrous results of civil war, or by the artificial political and economic barriers between East and West which become daily more formidable."

Two main problems concerned the European ecumenists: a new relationship with the German churches and with the churches in Eastern Europe or the Soviet occupied part of Europe.

Contacts with the German churches were established immediately after the war, in sharp contrast with the period after the First World War, when it lasted till after the Stockholm conference (1925) before the former enemies could meet each other(3). But contacts with the Confessing Church were never fully interrupted and these were now facilitated by the Stuttgart Declaration issued by the Fraternal Council of Evangelical Churches, in which Germany's guilt was openly confessed (August 8, 1945) and which at the same time was an expression of the sincere wish to come to a real renewal of the life of the church and its responsibility for society. Prof.J.B. Soucek from Prague said in a speech at the Nyborg Conference of European Churches (1959)(4) that the Confessing Church had been of great importance for the other churches in Europe, and that these had felt themselves associated with it in a common struggle. This had had positive results for the European ecumene. Through the initiative of the French army chaplain Marcel Sturm, the French-German Fraternal Council was formed in 1950(5). Others followed.

Unofficial groups, which tried, according to E. Emmen, the first president of the Conference of European Churches (6), over against the destructive powers of modern paganism which triumphed in the war, to bring together leading personalities of the Christian churches and in the light of the justice and reconciliation of Jesus Christ to cooperate in the reestablishment of Christian relations and in the recovery of the severely damaged body of Christ.

Präses E.D. Wilm saw the roots of the Conference of European Churches in the meetings of Dutch and German Christians(7). He and E. Emmen, the two architects of this European ecumenical organisation, met for the first time at the German-Dutch frontier near Sittard to speak about the problems connected with the annexation of German territory by the Dutch. In 1946 a delegation of the Netherlands Reformed Church visited Germany to establish contact with the German churches. The report mentioned already the danger of a return to the old confessional antitheses. In politics and in the church, reactionary tendencies were already emerging. The Stuttgart Declaration seems not to be representative for the real situation: and, therefore, found little response in the parishes. But a small group in leading positions did take very seriously the responsibility of the Christians for the life in church and society: and was trying to find new ways. The delegation found a great similarity between the spiritual crisis in the German churches and in their own church(8).

Not restoration but renewal was the guiding principle of those men and women who had been active in the Confessing Church and had rejected National-Socialism. But their influence would prove to be only partial. The political developments were such that restorative tendencies became dominant. The division of Germany into zones occupied by the Western allies and by the Soviet Union resulted in the creation of two German republics and the ecumenical dream of a German church renewed to unity and to a new consciousness of its social responsibility ended in a structural schism of protestant Germany and the existence of two church bodies, which mainly meet each other only at international church conferences.

The second ecumenical challenge was the establishment of contacts with the churches in Eastern Europe. The war period had given rise to a renewed interest in the Soviet Union. The common struggle against Fascism and the resurgence of the Russian Orthodox Church had fostered the hope that new developments lay ahead. Fritz Lieb, a Swiss theologian, a friend of Karl Barth, voiced what many felt in those days. In the preface of the Dutch edition of his book "Russland Unterwegs" (1945) he wrote:

"Our two countries cherish our tradition of freedom, but this should not keep us from looking towards the East and having an open eye for what the Soviet Union, although it has a totally different historical tradition and although much in its nature and actions is alien to us, has done for us in the common struggle against national-socialism and what Russia as a socialist state means for us and for our future." A visit to the Russian headquarters in Berlin in 1945, "gave me a new hope that a great future of friendly cooperation between the two powers for the sake of the reconstruction of a new Europe, lies ahead of us."

In his last chapter, he explains that his optimistic views on the developments in the Soviet Union are still only possibilities. But:

> "The Russian democracy is on its way, enormous creative powers in the spiritual field are active, a deep sense of human solidarity is awakening and with a differentiated attention for the spiritual faculties of the people, socialism is being built up."

Words from a now distant past!

But the book was widely read in the immediate post-war period and is in many ways typical for the expectations in European ecumenical circles. Especially the resurgence of the Russian Orthodox Church, after a long period of severe persecutions, which began with the historic meeting on September 4, 1943, between Stalin and the Metropolitains Sergy, Aleksy and Nikolay and the election of Sergy as the new Patriarch, were regarded as a clear sign of a steady amelioration in the situation of the church. The Archbishop of York, C. Garbett, was even present at his enthronement. The first foreign visitor of the Moscow Patriarchate and many were to follow! The European ecumene wanted to be a force of peace and reconciliation. The church has to be a pontifex - a bridge-builder - not a partisan, was the leading slogan of one of the German 'Kirchentage' (Berlin, 1949): and this might also be considered as the guiding principle of European ecumenical circles in their search for new relationships with Eastern Europe. This remained one of the main challenges for a considerable period: even to such an extent that the European ecumene has largely disregarded the process of integration of the (West)European nations.

A missed chance

The leading ecumenicals in the first decades after the war cannot be accused of having been dominated by anti-communist feelings and by cold-war attitudes. They have, on the contrary, always looked for openings towards Eastern Europe and for the development of new relations. Their concepts were more influenced by a pan-European than by a West-European vision. Roger Mehl said at one of the first meetings of the Conference of European Churches (a pan-European body):

> "The iron curtain is a reality, but for the sake of the Gospel, the churches in Europe have the obligation to profess openly that they will never recognize this great line of division and that they are never prepared to let themselves be hindered by it in their life."(9)

The last sentence does sound rather pretentious and has not been made true as the breaking up of the ties between the evangelical churches in Eastern and Western Germany some years later would confirm. But, as a whole, this quotation is typical for leading European ecumenical circles in that period. The beginning process of the West-European inter-state collaboration was for them not a real alternative and more regarded as a restorative initiative which would only deepen the division of the continent into two antagonistic blocs. The influence of the small group of German ecumenical Christians, who had their origin in the Confessing Church, seemed to have been quite determinative. They saw the main part of German protestantism cut off behind the Iron Curtain and were above all interested in the reunion of the two parts of Germany. A West-European bloc would only hamper a reunion which was still deemed possible: and might also lead to a further sovietisation of the other Eastern European countries. In the others, i.e. of the six countries which started to build up the West-European community, the influence of the ecumene was rather weak. Great Britain was not really interested. The British churches had not turned their attention to the continent in those days and were more directed towards the empire and the world-ecumene. They could only with the greatest difficulties be persuaded to join the Conference of European Churches in the sixties. Switzerland remained aloof from the process of West-European integration: as did the Scandinavian countries. Protestantism in Italy and Belgium forms only a very small minority; and French Protestantism, which showed a remarkable spiritual strength in the first decades after the war, was numerically too weak to exert a real influence on socio-political problems. An important part of the Dutch protestant world was still outside the ecumenical movement; and the ecumenical churchmen in the Netherlands Reformed Church were more interested in the pan-European than in the West-European relations in so far as their attention was not diverted by their own colonial problems.

No stimulating creative initiatives came forth from European ecumenical circles in the formation of a West-European supranational community. E. Gerstenmaier wrote in 1957(10): "German protestantism has not really given a programmatic contribution to a (West) European integration... and has been reluctant towards the concept of the European union in the last decade."

A West-European political union was, moreover, more in the line of the Roman Catholic church. Gerstenmaier mentions the opinion, widespread in protestant circles in those days, that the union of West-European countries as strived for in those days, was dominated by catholic countries and catholic concepts and would have disadvantageous consequences for the influence of Protestantism on public affairs. But he does not deem that this opinion has gained preeminence and he states that the 'small but active group around Heinemann and Niemöller who programmatically opposed the (West) European integration' had not been able to determine the policy of the church.

There was a sharp distinction between European ecumenical circles and the Roman Catholic Church in respect to their views on the relationship with Eastern Europe and the formation of a West European community. H. Stehle in his book 'Die Ostpolitik des Vaticans' (1975) wrote about the years 1949-1955 under the title: Auf Kaltem Krieg-Kurs (On a Cold War Course). And H. Brugmans, the Rector (1950-1972) of the College of Europe in Brugge, who converted to Catholicism in 1957, ended his book on the Crisis and Calling of the West (1952) with some remarks about the regimes of terror, the totalitarian society of Eastern Europe where the devil was on the run with all modern ideas. The Roman Catholics identified themselves with the union of Western Europe and contributed much more to its formation than the ecumenists in the protestant churches. At the same time, their attitude towards Eastern Europe was more controversial and aggressive. Cardinals like Mindszenty (Hungary) and Wyszynski (Poland) were the symbols of anti-communism, wide-spread in the Catholic Church in the West. Their opposition to the changes which took place in their society received wide support in the Catholic West. The protestant ecumene had quite different symbols. A man like J. Hromadka, who went a very long way in his understanding of the revolutionary changes in Eastern Europe and had great expectations of the new possibilities which these entailed, found a large audience in protestant ecumenical circles, although not without reservations. The West-European union was even regarded by some as retrogressive, as a reactionary concept, originating in a defensive attitude caused by a total misunderstanding of the real intentions of post-war communism.

The West-European ecumenical activists have largely disregarded the West-European socio-political developments; and, in those formative years, did not really engage themselves at all in the gradual rise of this new political and economic entity. This may be regarded in retrospect as a missed opportunity. The protestant ecumene has, as a result of this policy, not been able to build up a position from which the public witness of the churches could be heard and which would have enabled them to have an impact on the developments of the West European community of nations which was to develop into one of the most powerful economical forces in the world. In those days, when the ecumenical movement still had a rather large following in Europe and a lot of goodwill because of the role of the churches during the war in the occupied countries, it would have been possible to lay the foundations for a common organisation of the churches in the center of the West European community. But the chances have been missed and the possibilities not exploited. A Committee on the

Christian Responsibility for European Cooperation, under the chairmanship of André Philip and C.L. Patijn, had been formed in the fifties and started to issue a small bulletin in 1953. It was an unofficial ecumenical group of Christian laymen who wanted to engage European Christians in a discussion of European problems. The November 1958 Bulletin said: "It may well be that January 1, 1958 (when the Treaty of Rome began to be implemented) constitutes a turning point in the history of Western Europe. This event could have been taken more seriously by the European churches." But unfortunately it was not.

The Committee of laymen led to the foundation of the Ecumenical Commission for Church and Society in the European Community, which has a small office in Brussels. A weak instrument for churches which raise the claim that they have something to say about public affairs. They seem to neglect the simple fact that it is not only important to formulate the moral principles which should lead the social and political life of the nations, but that the ways and means should be created which make it possible that these principles are being listened to and can be applied in the field of practical politics. In the West-European community, the ecumenical churches have no strong voice which could be instrumental in making the witness of the churches in the social and political field a co-determining factor in the policy of the European community. The ecumene has, to a very large extent, closed its eyes to the formation of the West-European community. And, although the enlargement of the community has increased the number of protestant churches in the community, a creative ecumenical élan and the interest in European supra-national cooperation have largely disappeared. The ecumenical idea has lost its appeal to the people in Europe and protestant ecumenical witness in European affairs can be ignored by those in authority without the fear of losing their votes.

The West European ecumenists have not seen the coming into existence of their new context nor contributed to its creation. But they themselves are to blame if they have become irrelevant in the eyes of the new builders of Western Europe. The voice of the European ecumene was, for instance, completely absent in the Helsinki Continuation Conferences. But who could have taken the initiative to let the point of view and the concerns of the non-Roman Catholic churches be heard at these important European meetings? The Conference of (East and West) European Churches, which will be mentioned below, cannot speak with one voice; the churches in Eastern Europe cannot independently plead their cause at an international forum; and the West-European churches still have no well-structured common body to voice their interests. They continue to regard Geneva: i.e. the headquarters of the World Council of Churches, to a large extent as their own ecumenical organ. But Geneva is not the center of the European ecumene and declines to be identified with the West European ecumene. West European theologians speak a lot about contextual theology and about the witness of the churches in their concrete social situations: but, notwithstanding that, the West European member churches of the WCC have become almost voiceless and powerless in their own world. It might be an indication of very slight importance; but, nevertheless, it is rather significant that Geneva in no way stimulates initiatives to organize meetings of West European churches to discuss certain aspects of their ecumenical policy. Especially when these meetings concern their policy in the field of East-West relations. It is still so that a pan-European conception is the only one which seems to be acceptable in official ecumenical circles.

A resurgence of hope

The period of post-war reconstruction has shaped the ideals of those who have been prominent in the European ecumene. They may be blamed for not having discerned the inevitable course which the European development was taking and for having been too optimistic in their evaluation of the political developments in Eastern Europe. But they did have a vision which was worth striving for and a plan for a new Europe which was not just determined by the political realities of the day. We must not close our eyes to the fact that it was only a small group of people which was active on the European ecumenical scene. They have been able to take initiatives but have not succeeded in really exerting a determinative influence. In the churches restorative tendencies soon prevailed and the political develop-ments took a direction which made the pan-European concept rather unrealistic.

The East-West alliance which had defeated National-Socialism fell apart. The fate of Czechoslovakia and Hungary with which the protestant ecumenists had the closest relations, illustrates the ups and downs of the protestant ecumenists. The fashionable theory in the early years, that Czechoslovakia would become some kind of a bridge between East and West in the heart of Europe, received a severe blow with the final take-over by the communists in Prague in1948. The death of Jan Masaryk, who was found dead on the morning of 10 March 1948 in the courtyard of the ancient palace, in which his Ministry for Foreign Affairs was situated, symbolized the end of the liberal-democratic tradition in Eastern Europe. The course of the future developements had already become clear by the fact that as the result of strong pressure from Moscow, Czechoslovakia had to withdraw its initial acceptance for the Paris conference where the Marshall-plan for the economic recovery of Europe was to be discussed. In July 1947, a Czech delegation returned from Moscow and Masaryk told several friends afterwards: "I went to Moscow as the Foreign Minister of an independent sovereign state; I returned as a lackey of the Soviet government."(11)

The uprisings in Hungary in October 1956, where in the summer for the first time a meeting of the Central Committee of the World Council of Churches had taken place, and the occupation of Budapest by the Red Army on Sunday 4 November signified again that the political dreams of a greater and unified Europe, consisting of free and democratic nations, had become totally unrealistic. But, even if the vision of political and economic collaboration in Eastern and Western Europe was only short-lived and had come to naught, there still remained for the European ecumenists the obligation to care for the churches in Eastern Europe and to establish, where possible, fraternal relations with them. They were, during the fifties, almost the only people in the protestant churches who really cared for the churches in Eastern Europe and who constantly stressed the responsibility which the churches in East and West had for each other. In the protestant world, they were the only protagonists of religious liberty in Eastern Europe. In March 1951, the first issue of Background Information was published by the Study Department of the WCC, containing reports on the situation of the churches in the so-called Iron Curtain countries. From 1959 to 1967, Current Developments in the Eastern European Churches took over the information and documentation on Eastern Europe. A special commission on religious liberty was set up by the Central Committee (Nyborg 1958), which also published a bulletin with a review of the situation in many parts of the world: including the communist countries. These publications were neither inspired by anti-communism nor by unbrotherly feelings towards the churches; but they were a sign of solidarity with these churches who had gone through a very difficult time.

At the end of the sixties, the ecumene began to loose its interest in Eastern Europe: and the information about the situation of religious liberty gradually disappeared from the agenda.
But, although a realistic view of the factual situation prevailed, the ecumenists in Europe still hoped that changes for the good would be possible. Might it not be that after the death of Stalin (1953) and the unmasking of his regime of terror by Khrushchev a more liberal tendency would get the upperhand? It really seemed that changes for the good were taking place.

J. Hromadka had constantly pleaded for the collaboration of the ecumenical movement with the World Peace Council (1949). This, however, had been declined. The Commission of the Churches for International Affairs issued on 6 August 1951 a short statement which clarified the stance of the ecumene: "We condemn any extension of oppression, carried on behind the facade of propaganda for peace... "(12). In 1959 he took, together with the Czech Ecumenical Council, an initiative to bring the churches together in the Christian Peace Conference. The first ecumenical initiative in Eastern Europe and the first possibility for these churches to have a common meeting. It was clear that these meetings could easily be misused for political ends by those who had allowed them to start. The WCC was not enthusiastic; as it was feared that it could develop into a counter-movement to the World Council under the political dominance of the communist regime. But a meeting-place was created and a number of Western ecumenists were only too glad to be able to attend and to establish relations with those who had remained outside the ecumenical fellowship. The number of individual Western participants -the Western churches did not join the Christian Peace Conference- was increasing till the Third All-Christian Peace Assembly of April 1968, a most interesting gathering in the halcyon days of the Prague Spring. It seemed that, after all, there could be a possibility of a new beginning. Would, from Prague, in the heart of Europe, a new chapter in European history begin? Was the foundation laid for a regime which could be a bridge between the two antagonistic systems which divided our continent?

There was a resurgence of hope in the sixties. Under the influence of Pope John XXIII and the Vatican Council, the attitude of the Roman Catholic Church began to change; and the communist world seemed to be on the way towards a democratic, humanized form of socialism. Finally, a real dialogue could begin. Christians and Marxists seemed to have become aware of their need for each other and of their common responsibility for a world under the threat of nuclear disaster. Roger Garaudy, a leading French Marxist, subsequently expelled from the party, said at a congress of the Paulusgesellschaft in Salzburg: "The future of mankind cannot be built up either over against the faithful or without them; and the future of mankind cannot possibly be built up either in conflict with or without the communists."(13).

Although Roman Catholics played a leading role in this dialogue and Pope John's encyclical 'Pacem in Terris' (1963), which advocated a new approach to communism, contributed much to creating a new climate in which it could flourish, the contribution of Czech Protestantism was considerable. The Marxist philosopher Milan Machovec had a larg audience at the Karl-University in Prague. But also Josef Hromadka, once called 'the patriarch of the dialogue', and the Comenius-faculty had a determinative influence. Jan Milic Lochman described in his book 'Church in a Marxist Society'(14) the difficult way from anathema to dialogue:

"For us Christians this had two different aspects. One was a careful attempt to study what Marxism really was in its deepest possibilities and inspirations. This was not always easy- under the rule of a rather dogmatic and sterile form of orthodox Marxism with which we were confronted. But precisely in this respect it became our obligation not to identify the given ideological image with all posibilities of Marxism. In other words, we had to 'deideologize' the Stalinist version and to seek for Marxism's human, original and authentic face. In this effort, we developed a concentrated study of the young Karl Marx. It is interesting to note that the theologians started this study considerably earlier than the Marxists themselves. In the early fifties our Comenius Faculty in Prague was probably the only place in Eastern Europe where this deep humanistic philosophy was dealt with -as a challenge to the church first but also a challenge to that Stalinist form of Marxism which was then the only form officially recognized. We did it not against the Marxists, as an act of ideological battle; on the contrary, we did it for them- or better, in our common interest of humanization of our society and as a presupposition for future dialogue."

In the Czech town Marienbad the first dialogue conference in Eastern Europe took place in 1968, organised by the Paulusgesellschaft and the Czech Academy of Sciences. But 1968 also marked the end of this form of dialogue. No sadder illustration of this than the fact that the Czech Marxist sociologist Erika Kadlecova, who played such a decisive role in the preparation of this congress, and who, under Dubcek, was exhorted to establish a better relationship between the state and the churches, was later seen washing dishes in a Prague restaurant. Marxist orthodoxy pushed aside the revisionists who had taken part in the dialogue, and who had worked for renewal and for a breakthrough in a fossilized system and in the broken relations between Marxists and Christians who both wish to shape the future of Europe.

The conference of European Churches

But we must return to the end of the fifties. Even before Hromadka called together the Christian Peace Conference, Pastor E. Emmen, Secretary-General of the Netherlands Reformed Church and President E.D. Wilm of the Evangelical Church of Westphalia (Germany) had already taken the initiative to bring together some leading personalities from the churches to discuss how the relations between the churches, which had come about after the war, could be united in a common organization; and how better contacts with the sister churches in Eastern Europe could be established. This meeting in Brussels (1955) was followed by the first conference in Liselund (Denmark, 1957) with 62 participants. There it was decided to create 'a meeting-place and talkingshop' (15) for the European churches from East and West, which could contribute to reconciliation of the sharp political antitheses of the present and the age-old confessional divisions.

The churches of the reformation and the Orthodox churches had lived side by side for centuries in indifference, mutual distrust and mutual ignorance. Now, Orthodoxy should be drawn into an European ecumenical fellowship. This proved to have become possible. In the years between 1954-1959, a real renaissance of church life took place after the death of Stalin. M. Niemöller had visited Moscow in December 1951 and January 1952, called by W.A. Visser 't Hooft in his Memoirs(16) 'real pioneer's work'. A group of six representatives of the German churches under the leadership of G. Heinemann travelled to the Soviet Union in 1954, the Dutch Ecumenical Council visited the Soviet churches in June 1955, and the list of travellers to Moscow grew every year. The role of the German churches in the establishment of contacts with churches in the Soviet Union was very prominent. Professor L. Parijsky from the Leningrad Church Academy formulated in 1956 a number of questions about the principal points of disagreement between the Orthodox and Lutheran traditions, which he handed over to professor H. Iwand of Bonn. The beginning of the 'Arnoldshainer Gespräche', which started in October 1959, between representatives of the Evangelical Churches in Germany and the Russian Orthodox Church. They are continuing to this day and can probably be considered as the most important heritage of this period of pioneering in East-West relations. Here the theological dialogue to overcome the agelong process of alienation between Eastern and Western Christianity is really pursued in a consistent and responsible way, more or less aloof from political ups and downs and the interference of politically engaged fellow-Christians. The speech of E. Schlink at the Central Committee of the WCC at Rhodes in August 1959, 'The significance of the Eastern and Western Traditions for the Christian Church'(17) marked a turning-point. The Journal of the Moscow Patriarchate wrote: "None of the Protestants has as yet spoken about Orthodoxy in this way."(18)

The Orthodox were open to contacts with the churches of the Reformation: and the main Lutheran churches were willing to cooperate. The greatest difficulty in those years was to draw the British churches into the Conference of European Churches which held its first official meeting in Nyborg (Denmark) in 1959: incidentally, the reason why these meetings were originally called Nyborg Conferences. Among the 90 participants were 18 delegates from Eastern Europe and 20 from East and West Germany. No less than 27 of the participants were either advisers or observers from Christian organisations of youth, the press and lay-centers. The theme was: European Christianity in the present, secularized world, which give a good indication of the current idea that the secularisation process was common to both East and West and that it could be useful to come to a common understanding of the task and mission of the church. The author of this essay has the most impressive memories of Nyborg IV in 1964.

Because of political difficulties, and to ensure the partici- pation of the participants from Eastern Germany, the conference was held on the M.S. Borholm, sailing in international waters around Denmark. The East German delegates were brought aboard in a small vessel from a Swedish port. The European ecumene could not find another meeting-place, but was not prepared 'to let itself be hindered in its life by the great line of division'. Was not the ecumenical symbol a ship on the rough waters of world history? There was a feeling of satisfaction. Politics and ideologies may try to separate us from each other; but we defy the powers of hatred and antagonism and break through the Iron Curtain for the sake of reconciliation and renewal.

The Nyborg V Assembly was held in Portschach (Austria) in 1967 to avoid the difficulties for the GDR delegation to attend. Yet, part of the delegation had not been allowed to attend the meeting which was held under the theme: A Task for the Churches in Europe: to serve and reconcile. This was introduced by a prerecorded, but brilliant speech of W.A. Visser 't Hooft, General-Secretary of the WCC (1948-1966), who was himself prevented by the illness of his wife from appearing at the conference.(19)

He challenged the churches by asking if they really were on the way to discover together what it meant in the Europe of the 1960s to concentrate their whole life on service and reconciliation and he outlined five specific tasks for the churches to undertake in their mission of reconciliation:
1. To transform outdated church structures into channels of service and reconciliation;
2. The church should manifest itself as the family of recon- ciled servants. If the European churches thought and lived as one body, they would not be so lukewarm about real unity in faith and order as they are today. They would take their important decisions together;
3. The provision of the motivation and dynamic for a world- wide policy of development;
4. Pioneering ways of overcoming tensions between East and West. The churches are called to reconcile, but in the case of Europe there are specific reasons why the churches have a unique task of bridge-building, because the present division of Europe has been prepared and aggravated by the breach between Eastern and Western Christianity. They must seek to help the nations and ideologies to break through old taboos,

to make a new beginning through forgiveness of the wrongs of the past and to take up together the new common tasks;
5. To show 'the other face of Europe'. In the life of Europe there has not only been a tradition of lust for power and domination, but also a tradition of service and reconciliation. There was another face of Europe. There was a cloud of witnesses who pointed to the humble and humiliated Christ. There was St. Francis with his poverty, Pascal with his knowledge of the scandal of the Cross, Rembrandt with his portrayal of the Jesus who emptied himself, Kierkegaard with his incognito, Dostojewski with the Christ whose victory over the Grand Inquisitor was a victory of suffering love, Bonhoeffer who preached and paid the cost of discipleship, Simone Weil who sought to share the suffering of Christ.

A most inspiring message; but, as the British chronicler of the conference remarked, it soon got lost beneath a pile of papers and in a stream of verbal clichés. It must unfortunately be said that this has happened with most of the other inspiring incentives, meant to enliven the common ecumenical endeauvours of the European churches. The Polish Lutheran Bishop Michelis pleaded in Liselund in 1957 for the creation of a lively, prophetic organ of European Christians, a sort of European 'Kirchentag' according to the German model. But the Conference of European Churches has, in the course of time, developed into a rather formalistic-ecclesiastical stucture with 108 member churches in 26 European countries. The European lay-movements have not been integrated and founded their own inter-European meetings. So did the youth-movements which turned away from a body in which high ecclestiastics were calling the tune. Missionary and other church-organisations did not decide to use the CEC as their European platform. Contacts with the Conference of European Bishops conferences have been established since a common meeting in Chantilly (France) in April 1978; but this has not given new impulses to the Conference.

The constant East-West tensions, the formalistic hierarchical character of the Orthodox churches, and the absence of lay-initiatives and of Christian organisations in most Eastern European countries have strongly marked the development of the CEC.
It has remained in the margins of the life of the churches, probably best illustrated by the small office it occupies in the WCC building in Geneva. The causes of the stagnation of the development of the CEC and of the reason why it has not been able to occupy a more prominent place in European churchlife can be summarized under the heading '1968'.

1968 and thereafter

The year 1968 can, in many respects be regarded as a turning-point in the ecumene in Europe. In the first place it confirmed the decline of the central position of the European churches in the ecumenical movement. The WCC Assembly at Uppsala (Sweden) made it clear that from now on Third World churches would set the pace. Their problems and their priorities would determine the life of the ecumene, which had become more diversified and less surveyable, more complicated and less monochrome. Europe should see to its own problems and not make them the ecumenical priori-ties of the whole world church. Anti-colonialism and the new selfconsciousness of the young nations marked a new generation of their church representatives. The anti-racism programme, which concentrated on white racism, was given a prominent place. A moratorium on all Western aid and the influence which this entailed, was proposed; although it was not really put into practice for obvious reasons. The Western welfare society seemed to be definitely established and did it not again accentuate the new imperialism and lust for power of the old continent? The European ecumenists, who had always regarded the World Council of Churches as their natural milieu and considered the acceptance of their ideas, priorities and way of life as a matter of course, began to feel ill at ease in this new situation. A new type of ecumenist began to emerge. The liberals began to give way to the radicals. These qualifications should not be taken in a political or confessional sense, but are used to denote the type of perso-nalities. 'Cardinals' like Monsieur Marc Boegner (de l'Academie Française!) were succeeded by 'development-workers'. No new pioneers took over their torch when, after 25 years, the genera-tion, deeply stamped by war experiences and postwar ideals of European renewal, was gradually leaving the ecumenical scene. Those who replaced them had another outlook on the world and the way its problems should be tackled. Not reconstruction but revolution, a new justice inspired by a new world-solidarity became the dominating trend. This was not the climate in which traditional European churchmen and theologians felt at home. The European ecumenists began to concentrate on the study and docu-mentation of the ecumenical movement, but were, not always very gently, moved to the side-line of the ecumenical fellowhip. In the churches themselves an ecumenical inertia and the impact of an ongoing secularisation process began to be felt. The new prosperity certainly did not stimulate the spiritual life. As the Pilgrim Fathers once remarked: Religion brought forth Prosperity, but the Daughter ultimately devoured the Mother.

The original élan had come to a standstill. Too many ecumeni-cal initiatives had ebbed away and too many promises had remained unfulfilled on the European ecumenical scene. Restoration not renewal was what church people were observing, and, most likely, expecting. The Roman-Catholic churches which in the post-war period had remained outsiders, were quickly making up their arrears in the sixties. And, although a reaction soon set in, this period has clearly shown that only in close cooperation and fellowship with Roman Catholics can there be a new future and a new start for the European ecumene.

Yet another event characterized the year 1968 and put an end to dreams of renewal. On August 21 the Soviet tanks again entered Prague. This time they did not come as liberators as in 1945: but as oppressors.
J. Hromadka protested and expressed in a letter to the Soviet Ambassador in Prague his 'deepest feelings of disillusionement, sorrow and shame.'
The ecumene equally raised a sharp but impotent protest. The events in Prague signified the end of an epoch of ecumenical aspirations in the field of East-West relations. Some of the previous initiatives continued: but did not contribute much to the life of the churches.

The Christian Peace Conference passed through a deep crisis: and, when it resurged in 1971, it had lost its open-forum character.(20)
A CPC publication (21) gave a completely new self-portrait and a new set of marching orders. The 'new, determinedly anti-imperialistic orientation' was formulated in five theses:
1. The CPC is no pluralistic discussion club. Christians may not remain neutral in the current conflict between differing social systems. The CPC considers itself a partial, action society of Christians for peace.
2. The CPC disagrees with the opinion that the commandment of Christians is to follow in principle a 'third way' leading between the fronts. A manifestation of this principle is the debate concerning the 'correct socialism'.
3. The struggle for peace must today be conducted as a struggle against imperialism, since only in the latter can the structures of peaceful coexistence and social justice be asserted.
4. The conflict between the East and the West cannot be
   replaced by a North-South conflict, but both are interconnec-
   ted as a conflict for social justice (...).
5. Peace can only be established on the basis of peaceful
   coexistence among states with differing social systems. Coexistence is a conception of the struggle against imperialism and it also implies creating the necessary room for anti-colonial liberation movements. The CPC disagrees with the opinion that the Christian ministry of reconciliation obliges it to support a convergence of both world systems or a 'democratization' of socialism.

The Third World became the main field of action of the CPC, where it operates as an instrument of propaganda for Marxist Socialism. The East-West dimension receded into the background and the ecumene expanded to include other religions, as it did in all other Eastern European peace-initiatives.

Prague 1968 also signified the end of the Christian-Marxist dialogue in the form in which it had just started. A new concept of dialogue was propagated from Eastern Europe, which would not endanger their system and would prevent any Western influences in the intellectual and social sphere. Dialogue became a synonym for practical collaboration with the communists, a collaboration which presupposes the acceptance of the 'objectively based' leading role of the Communist Party and its Central Committee. The dialogue was now seen as an instrument for the attainment of specific political objectives, which must be fitted exclusively into the ideological framework of one of the partners and as an active force in the struggle against imperialism.

The most important official pronouncement on dialogue was made at the International Communist Conference held in Moscow in 1969. The Party announced:

"In various countries co-operation and joint action between communists and the broad democratic masses of Catholics and believers of other religions is developing. It has acquired great urgency. The dialogue between them on such problems as war and peace, capitalism and socialism, neo-colonialism and the developing countries, joint action against imperialism and for democracy and socialism, is very pressing. Communists are of the opinion that on this path -the path of broad contacts and joint activities- the mass of believers is becoming an active force in the struggle against imperialism and for thorough social transformation."

The only possible commentary on such a statement was already formulated in 1962 by Cardinal König from Vienna(22). Dialogue cannot be reduced to practical collaboration, because:

"It would be against the dignity of the human person as a spiritual being, it would be inhuman if Christians were asked to consent to and to cooperate with a social structure, whether existing or to be built (a socialist or communist structure), without their being given permission and the opportunity to scrutinize this structure by means of a dialogue between equals."

But the policy of the Party was going to be clearly determined by the 1969 resolution and most churches under their domination could do nothing else than let themselves be fitted into this conception of collaboration. They were allowed to participate in international ecumenical work, but pressured into a complete conformity whenever these activities touched upon political questions. W.A. Visser 't Hooft had once written(23):

"Communist policy is not the extermination of the churches but their domestication. They are allowed to exist if they will in no way go against the policies of the government and stick to that very restricted field of activity which religion should occupy according to the Marxist view."

Later on, these domesticated churches, which in the interior cannot unfold any activity in the social and political field, were actively enlisted for the support of national purposes abroad. And this got a real extension and intensification after 1968.

The Conference of European Churches has been less directly affected by Prague 1968 than the CPC, but certainly began to feel a stronger impact from the Soviet churches. One gets the impression that the Soviets, too, consider it as an ecclesiastical body which has but little bearing on the life of the churches and which for that reason does not raise their special interest.
  At the Nyborg VI Assembly (1971), prof. N.A. Zabolotsky from the USSR, speaking about the future work of the Conference, said(24):

"The churches of the Eastern socialist countries... will manifestly continue to strive for the following objective: to make their voice clearly heard with the Conference and to have it accepted on equal terms, for it reflects the consciousness and desires of very many believers who are simultaneously builders of the new social and political relations in Europe."

It is implied in such a statement that the consciousness and the desires of the believers among the builders of the new social and political relations in Europe are voiced by the party through its Central Committee, which is the only organ to express what people want (i.e. what they are dictated to want). The Russian Orthodox Church has no other possiblity than to act as a protagonist of the political line of the government.
Zabolotsky also indicated:

"two directions for the work of the CEC, deserving the support of the Russian Orthodox Church: theology and action for peace... dialogue must have a theological side (the building up among Christians of one mind in faith, hope and love) and a peace-making side (practical service, namely peaceful coexistence, cooperation and development for the good of all)."

This proposal has determined the work of the CEC ever since. It held its Assemblies in 1974 (Engelberg, Switzerland) and in 1979 (Crete) and the next Assembly, which has been repeatedly postponed, is now scheduled for October 1986 in Edinburgh. The main activities, however, are concentrated on the organisation of small study-consultations (five in the period 1979-1983) on such subjects as how the problems of peace are related to the understanding of the Trinity (1982); ecumenical relationships in Europe and peace questions (1981); spirituality, ecology and peace. The theme of the 1986 Assembly will be: Glory to God and Peace on Earth.

Zabolotsky's proposals still determine the agenda. Two new initiatives were taken in 1980: a Consultative Committee on Islam in Europe was set up and a three years old proposal to form a Human Rights Working Committee (to be continued till December 1986) could finally be realised. The name 'Working' Committee is a bit misleading as most emphasis is being put on study.

In this field of human rights the predicament of East-West collaboration of the churches becomes quite clear. They cannot deal together in an open, critical and prophetic way with these problems. The situation in Europe is too contradictory. In one part, the human rights situation can be regarded as unique in the world, with even a special court in Strasbourg with supranational authority, to which individual citizens can adress themselves, and churches which have every possibility to deal with human rights issues in the theoretical and practical field. In the other part, the human rights situation is abominable without any possibility for the churches either for a free theoretical discussion or for practical interventions. The CEC can neither disregard the problem nor deal with it in a relevant way. Consultations about the subject thus produce statements on education for peace as a task for the churches; always useful but when not specified in detailed programmes and methods rather irrelevant (educational problems in general, although a burning issue for all Christians in Eastern Europe, are never discussed!), or repeat what has been said over and over again, but does unfortunately not determine the policy of all European governments, that religious liberty constitutes an essential element of human rights(25). One can hardly suppose that conclusions reached at other study-meetings are suprisingly new for the churches in Europe: a meeting expressed that the problem of efficiency in the churches' involvement in human rights, intercession, prayer and pastoral work were key-elements and a meeting of mainly Orthodox Churches gave a reminder of the pastoral and worship dimension of human rights.

The Conference of European Churches has not developed, after 1968, as an organisation for which church people in the West are showing any real interest. After a visit to Scandinavia, the

General-Secretary wrote(26): "The work of CEC was completely unknown and barely understood in Scandinavia." But this does not only apply to the Scandinavian churches, which contributed so much to the Nyborg (!) conferences, but also to many churches. Outside the 'church-chancelleries' nothing is known about it: and, even there, it is usually only a topic for discussion when a delegate to a consultation must be chosen. A current suspicion is that one of the main criteria then is: who is available and has deserved a nice trip abroad.

In theological reviews, the CEC is never discussed. Initiatives taken by the Interchurches Peace Council in the Netherlands for a European Peace Platform -rejected by the GDR churches as unrealistic in the present situation- have completely ignored the CEC. Nobody has even thought of using it for this purpose. The specific task of the churches in powerful economic entities as the Comecon and the EEC is never discussed. The incomparable position of the churches in these communities makes such a discussion in this forum impossible and quite useless. The impact of the CEC on European public life is negligible and can be summarized in a sentence from the scanty CEC Newsbulletin(27): The meeting 'expressed deep concerns and profound hope'. If the Conference of European Churches is a criterion of the ecumenical élan in Europe, the conclusion cannot be very optimistic.

The morning after the dream before

M.J. Le Guillou (28) remarked that contacts between Eastern and Western Christianity, which had come about in the long centuries of separation and mutual ignorance, have always remained 'sans lendemain' (without a tomorrow). It is equally true that the origin and the continuation of the Great Schism (1054) have been strongly influenced by political factors. A survey of church history gives no cause for optimism: and, when one takes a realistic view of the present situation, one can easily come to the conclusion that the same applies to the post-war developments in Europe. The political situation determines to a large extent the relations of the churches in Europe and awakening from the post-war ecumenical dream we find a divided continent, containing two antagonistic political blocs with an ongoing social and cultural estrangement. Will our ecumenical contacts again prove to be 'sans lendemain'? That would be a really tragic situation, for we must not forget that after World War II the content of the notions East and West has changed rather dramatically. With the term Eastern Europe we cannot any longer denote that part of our continent where the Orthodox Churches are the main confession. The political notion of Eastern Europe, as it is used now, includes countries which, in a cultural and confessional sense, are traditionally part of the West. The dominating influence of the Soviet Union and, in its train, of the Russian Orthodox Church, whose dream of being 'The Third Rome' seems in a rather unexpected way to be realized in our days, will assure that tensions between Orthodoxy and the Western churches will have a strong bearing on the relationships with the other churches in the Eastern political block. A small illustration of this dominating position, which might reveal more than a complete description of the many activities of the Russian Orthodox Church in Eastern Europe, are the receptions in East-Berlin of the residing Russian Bishop, twice a year at Easter and on the occasion of the name-day of the Patriarch.

At these receptions, in a grand bourgeois style, the authorities of church and state are invited and speeches are exchanged about friendship, mutual understanding and brotherly collaboration between our nations as the presupposition of lasting peace (29). The Byzantinism which has crept into the European ecumene remains an interesting phenomenon for many a post-war ecumenical fieldworker!

We must take into account that an East-European form of ecumenical collaboration is developing with regular consultations which are intended to unify the policy of the churches in the socialist countries. The Russian Orthodox Church does play a prominent role in this process and there are enough indications to assume that the State-Secretariat for Religious Affairs equally exerts an influence. The prospects of a pan-European ecumenical collaboration of the churches are indeed not very bright.

Some modest suggestions for a policy of our churches may close this essay.

a. The role and the possibilities of the churches in the two socio-political systems, which devide our continent, are so different that it is quite impossible to arrive at a commonly - held, independent position with respect to the many questions which the churches are concerned with at this moment. It is even the case that "The same words have a different consonance depending on the respective political contexts."(30)

Section IV of the Pörtschach Assembly said:

"When we come to describe what it means to live under the Lordship of Christ in the realm of politics, as a group we do not know what to say. The reason for this is that our environments are so diverse, our pre-suppositions so different, that we find it impossible to define a specially Christian responsibility in a meaningful, comprehensive manner."

In the light of this, it might be advisable to concentrate in our pan-European relations on theological issues in the way in which these are treated in the 'Arnoldshainer Gespräche' or in the 'Leuenberger Gespräche' between the Lutheran and Reformed Churches. The Conference of European Churches should maintain the low profile which it maintains at present in the European ecumene. It should remain 'a meeting-place and talking shop' without any eagerness to speak out on the social and political evils of the day. The organization of small study-consultations without any public pretensions should be continued. It might not be possible to prevent large assemblies from being held. The pressures to which such meetings are usually exposed to make prophetic pronouncements on public issues can have very harmful, divisive effects. The relations between the churches of Eastern and Western Europe are too fragile to take any risks.

b. The West European churches are still confronted with the problem of creating the necessary structures through which their witness and service can function within the steadily expanding (West) European community. The Ecumenical Commission of the Churches for questions of Church and Society in Brussels appealed to the churches in the Community in 1982 to strengthen their presence at the European institutions in Strassburg and Brussels. This appeal should be taken to heart. Certain aspects of church and society relations have to be considered in the context of the Community as a whole: and no longer within the framework of individual nations. This should not be regarded as a social conformism to the powers that be.
The churches should not present themselves as a kind of social cement which can hold the community together; neither should they forget about their partners in Eastern Europe. But the West-European churches should finally take their own context seriously and realize that whatever contribution they can make to show the 'other face' of Europe can in the present circumstances, only be given within the context of their own larger society.

NOTES

1. Les Clandestins de Dieu, Cimade 1939-1945, Paris 1968
2. Ecumenical Review Vol. III, Jan. 1951, p. 163
3. See: History Ecumenical Movement, Geneva 1954, p. 536. Beginnings of German Cooperation.
4. Die Europäische Christenheit in der heutigen Welt. Nyborg 1959, Zürch 1960, p. 106.
5. Bekennende Kirche, München 1952, p. 309. According to Roger Mehl: Das protestantische Europa, Zürich 1959, p. 25, the French-German Fraternal Council was formed in Amsterdam 1948.
6. Bericht Konferenz Europäischen Kirchen. Liselund 27-31 Mai 1957, p. 18
7. Liselund, p. 80
8. Handelingen Generale Synode der Nederlandse Hervormde Kerk ten jare 1946, p. 460
9. Liselund, p. 39
10. Dokumente - Zeitschrift für übernationale Zusammenarbeit, 13.Jhrg. Juni 1957
11. Zbynek Zeman - The Masaryks, 1976, p. 208
12. J.A. Hebly, The Russians and the World Council of Churches, Belfast 1978, p. 68.
13. J.A. Hebly, All is now quiet in Marienbad. Christopher Read, The Soviet attitude to the christian.marxist dialogue. Religion in Communist Lands, Vol. I, no. 6 1973, p.4-12
14. New York, 1970, p. 179
15. Michael De-la-Noy, A task for the Churches in Europe, Geneva 1968, p. 23
16. Dutch edition 1971, p. 235
17. Ec. Review Vol. XII. 1960, p. 130-142
18. Herder Korrespondenz XIV, p. 268
19. De-la-Noy, p. 16
20. Albert Boiter, The Christian Peace Conference: 1958-1983. A political overview. Paper presented at the AAASS National Convention in Kansas City, October 1983.
21. Ingo Boer, Christian Peace Conference. Prague 1974, p. 50-51
22. "Some theories on the Christian-Marxist Dialogue", Bolletino del segretariato per i non credenti. No. 2, June 1962, p. 8-15
23. Christianity and Crisis, July 1949
24. This happened at Nyborg VI, Geneva, p. 42, 43
25. Press Release Workshop 1984, Eisenach GDR; CEC News 1984-17 and 11.
26. CEC News 1977-13
27. CEC News 1983-7.
28. Mission et Unité, 1960 I, p. 154
29. See f.i. Stimme der Orthodoxie 1979-7, p. 19; 1979-12, p. 17
30. Chr. Hintz of the GDR during a consultation held at Sofia, 1978. Occasional Paper no. 10, p. 71.

Chapter III

CHURCHES IN EASTERN EUROPE: THREE MODELS OF CHURCH—STATE
RELATIONS AND THEIR RELEVANCE FOR THE ECUMENICAL MOVEMENT

It is not so easy to define exactly what we mean when we
speak of 'Eastern' Europe. Geographically the notion is rather
unclear; the GDR and Hungary, for instance do not consider
themselves belonging to Eastern Europe in this sense.
Confessionally we speak of the Eastern and Western churches,
meaning Latin and Orthodox Christianity, and in this sense Poland
belongs to the West. For present purposes let us speak of Eastern
Europe in the popular political sense; namely, that part of a
continent which has a communist system of government and belongs
to the Soviet sphere of influence. In that sense Yugoslavia is
not really part of Eastern Europe.

It is also a very complicated matter to speak in general
about 'the' churches in Eastern Europe. Every church has its own
history and background. There are those which have been up until
modern times powerful, privileged people's-churches and which
have gone through a difficult process of adaptation to a totally
new situation. Then, there are small minority churches, often
oppressed in the past, which were at first inclined to accept a
new communist regime as a sort of liberation from age-long
oppression by ruling confessions. There are Orthodox, Roman
Catholic, Lutheran and Reformed churches that have reacted in
their own, very different ways to the situation that arose after
the communists had taken over. The relations of church and state
and church and society were and are not identical, and the fact
that the communist regime was established in the Soviet Union in
1917 and in the other countries only after 1945 is not without
significance. The communists initially tried to apply the Soviet
mother—model of church—state relations in the other countries,
but that has in some cases been a complete failure, most clearly
in the GDR and in Poland. It is for that reason impossible to
speak in general terms about the church in socialism, or the
church in Eastern Europe. One should always be more specific in
defining historical and confessional contexts.

Another important factor which should be kept in mind is that
there has been a process of development in church—state relations
in the last 30 years. It no longer suffices to speak of a general
policy of persecution and oppression of the church. There have
been changes in the policy or tactics of the regimes. They have
learned to live with the fact that Christian churches continue to
exist and that they will do so for a considerable time. In the
ideal communist society, belief in God and the church will have
died, but this stage has not yet been reached and, as some
communists say, the disappearance of religion is not a condition

for, but will be a consequence of the establishment of a communist society.

The present stage, that of 'developed real' socialism, is not longer regarded solely as a transitory period, a sort of purgatory before entering paradise. The myth of progress has fallen into the background. Communism, as Wolfgang Büscher writes, is not so much political action directed toward conquering and establishing political power,

"but a form of the existing society aimed at stabilization. It is establishment. In spite of all present polemics against the thesis of Ulbricht of socialism as a relatively independent form of society between capitalism and communism, this thesis is the hidden ideological basis of present party policies. An inspiring concept of progress and a model of the future which can mobilize the workers and the intellectuals are wanting in GDR socialism. It is more a question of the stabilization of existing conditions(1)."

The party wants the churches as supporting partners, the ideology has not succeeded in really inspiring the people, and the party looks for those elements which can help build up a new national identity. The celebration of the Luther Year in the GDR is a good example. The regime has come to the conclusion that there should be a constructive 'miteinander von Staat und Kirche' (a togetherness of state and church). The Hungarian Reformed Bishop Károly Tóth says that the Marxists themselves discover that improvement of social conditions does not automatically create the new person, but rather emphasizes the problems of individual life. Because of this he sees new dimensions for the pastorate of the church in present-day Hungarian society(2).

Because of the endeavors to bring in the churches as associates for the building up of the real socialistic society, anti-church policies and aggressive atheist propaganda have been abandoned in the GDR and Hungary. Fundamentally, a similar tendency can be observed at work in the Soviet Union. The existence of the church is more or less accepted or tolerated and the fight against religion is in some publications presented as a fight against those social roots from which religion arises. If the social causes of religious consciousness are eliminated, then this changes it into a tree without roots, which withers away and perishes(3). In the Soviet Union, however, there is a distinct tendency to encourage this process of decay and there is active propaganda for atheism. It is said in an article in Pravda:

"Since the establishment of a new social order the tendency toward the decay of religion in the USSR is strengthening. It would be a mistake, however, to assume that religious faith can fully disappear on its own, only through the influence of the socialist way of life and the achievements of technical-scientific progress, (or) without the development of systematic, efficient atheistic work(4)."

This should not, however, have only the form of enlightenment, but be directed towards the activation of the participation of believers in the society in the existing social, political and cultural organizations. V. Kuroyedov wrote in Kommunist:

"The involvement of believers in the practical struggle of the building up of socialism and communism, and at the same time the constant propaganda for the materialistic world-view among the masses, is the scientifically correct way to overcome religious prejudices(5)."

A description follows of the church-state situation in three socialist countries: The Orthodox Church in the USSR, and the Protestant churches in Hungary and in the GDR- three different models. The Russian Orthodox Church (ROC) is above all a priestly church, which seeks solidarity with people and nation, stresses the liturgical-sacramental life, and does not deal with social and political issues on its own impulse but only where the government expects it. This is the case especially in peace work. The ROC adopts a patriotic, not an ideological, position. The leaders of the Hungarian Protestant churches identified themselves with the ruling regime and accepted the place which the regime accords them. The Council of Evangelical Churches in the GDR wants to be loyal to socialism, but is constantly involved in a struggle for the safeguarding of its right to exercise its prophetic ministry and to speak out independently on vital questions in the life of the nation. In describing these three models, I do not want to suggest that there exist only these. We should always endeavor as noted above, to give a nuanced view of the church-state relations in the different national and confessional contexts. And by choosing these three models I just wish to illustrate the variety of these relationships.

The Russian Orthodox Church

There seem to be two apparently contradictory tendencies in the policies of the Soviet government and the ruling CPSU in regard to the church, which we could describe with the words marginalization and integration. Both these words have a special meaning and content in this context. Marginalization means that the church is only allowed to move in a strictly religious-liturgical sphere and not to intrude in other aspects of the life of the society. Its task is to satisfy the religious needs of the faithful. This is implied in the legislation which is very restrictive as far as those aspects of religious liberty are concerned which do not directly relate to the celebration of the liturgy. The decree on separation of church and state is interpreted in such a way that the church is separated from society and that it has no right to have anything to do with cultural, social or political questions or to display any activities in these fields. The church has become absolutely marginal in regard to society and a Soviet citizen will not encounter the church in any province of daily life. But there are two more aspects which give this marginalization a special Soviet coloration. The first is that the party and government see it as their task to exercise an anti-religious influence especially by means of education, publicity, press and propaganda. In Soviet terminology this is called enlightenment to liberate the people from the influence of unscientific ideas. This causes an alienation of believers from society. Their own contribution to the life of the nation is disqualified in advance and there is no right of defense or reply, because this is forbidden by law as propaganda for the faith.

A second aspect of marginalization is that this does not mean that the church may live its own life in silence in a quiet corner of society. The authorities exercise sharp control over the life of the church through their Council for Religious Affairs; they interfere in the inner life of the church and they are motivated by a deep animosity toward the church. Interference in the life of the church was a normal procedure in Tsarist times, too. Those observers who accept the thesis that a traditional authoritarian system of government is today perpetuating itself in a new quasi-socialist form can find strong support in their favor in the attitudes of the government towards the church. An essential difference of course, is the fact that the present government does not only want to arrange the affairs of the church, but that it does this with intention of putting a brake on the life of the church, to hinder, damage, and abolish it.

The other tendency of Soviet policies in regard to the church could be called integration. They want to use the church for the building up of socialism. In Soviet terminology the revolutionary workers movement within real socialism has the task to strengthen and deepen the unity of action between representatives of the Marxist-Leninist world-view and religiously believing people in the process of building socialism(6).

Since 1943 the Soviet regime has gradually started taking into account the fact that it is not all that easy to destroy the church and that an increasing number of citizens intend to stick to their convictions. The realization began to break through that it could be useful to make the church subservient to national political purposes, as, for instance, the strengthening of the inner cohesion of the socialist world, the re-establishment of the Soviet influence in the Middle East and, since the 1950s, the Soviet peace offensive. The ROC proved to be a useful and docile instrument, but the regime remained cautious lest the influence and position of the church in the life of the country should increase in any way. (One recalls the extreme form of marginalization, an active campaign of church persecution during the Khrushchev period). The peace activities of the church are thus directed mainly towards churches and people abroad.

The Council for Religious Affairs has the special duty to 'help' the church; that is to say, this state office controls its activities and defines their content. The aim of the regime is to demonstrate abroad that the communists are willing to cooperate with believers. Anti-religious actions appeared to impede the influence of communism among traditionally believing people in Muslim and Third World countries, so the intention is now to establish the image of positive collaboration of communists and believers and of real religious liberty under socialism. The adherence of the ROC to membership in the World Council of Churches (WCC) in 1961 also was motivated by the government, which gave the green light for this step in a period of great internal tension between church and state, to play a role in the worldwide ecumenical movement because of the possibilities which WCC membership offered for the furtherance of the peace movement (Peace is identified with the establishment of socialism) and for the furtherance of the policies of the socialist motherland.

The integration of the church and the believers in Soviet society must not be seen as a process in which they can bring their own values and ideas about the human being and society in the building of socialism. It is rather a process of assimilation in which they should be liberated from their antiquated, unscientific views; it is an enforced conformism in an ideologically synchronized society. The Christians may participate only when they keep silent about their own social and ethical principles and take part in peace work whose aims and principles have been determined without their collaboration or influence.

There is an inward immigration and an outward conformism of believers and the church is involved in a constant and bitter struggle for its life. This struggle is not characterized by a militant and active confrontation with or opposition against the regime, although militant groups do exist. The struggle of the church is rather characterized by a strong commitment to its spiritual traditions, by perseverance in the faith, and a quiet building up of the pastoral life of the church. These are the weapons with which the church responds to marginalization. It perseveres in silence under the atheistic propaganda and suffers humbly the interference of the secular powers in its life. The church, and especially the ROC, realizes that its real power does not lie in official public recognition and an efficient organization of church life, but in the devotion, the fidelity and the sacrifice of many millions of believers, The church cannot reach out to these people, but they come to it and support it.

The ROC also has not resisted the integration enforced by the regime. It has accepted it, but at the same time has tried to make it serve its own position in a way that is not always in accord with the regime's intentions. The willingness to collaborate with the building of socialism, according to leading hierarchs, is based on the assumption that the party realizes in practice the righteousness which was preached by Christ. Communism is in this way reduced to a byproduct of Christianity, with the further implication that the party only practices what always has been preached by the church.
The ideological pride of a scientific world-view is wounded by such suggestions. They touch Soviet ideologists at a vulnerable spot.

Collaboration with the regime is also motivated by the fervent patriotism which has always been characteristic of the Russian Orthodox Church. It has always been on the side of the people and so it is now; it sings in concert the praises of the Great October Revolution, the Great Patriotic War, and the achievements of socialism. The ROC stresses its contribution in periods of need and of threat to the life of the nation. It integrates itself in a way that disturbs the ideologists. In Nauka i Religiia, the way in which the ROC is preparing for the celebration in 1988 of the millenial anniversary of the baptism of Vladimir was sharply attacked; it said:

"One should refute the church legends about certain historic facts and figures and the pretensions of church organizations that proclaim themselves bearers of the patriotic principle and guardian of the spiritual heritage of the nation."(7)

The way in which the church tries to use its enforced integration to reinforce its own position seems to be regarded as menacing by Soviet authorities. It must also be acknowledged that not all bishops accept the integration in the same manner. There are degrees in loyalty as even the Furov report, a secret Soviet government report about the church, published in 1980 in the West, clearly shows.

Integration in the peace offensive and in propaganda abroad is also regarded by the church as a means of survival and strenghtening its position. It must be acknowledged, however, that the ROC, especially in this aspect of its activities, tends

46

to put the sister churches with which relations are maintained in a rather awkward position and to raise a number of problems for the ecumenical movement which have scarcely been analyzed up till now.

The Hungarian Model

The Reformed Bishop Tibor Bartha spoke in 1968 about the development of a specific Hungarian model of cooperation between the churches and the socialist state. He alluded to the Reformed and Lutheran churches, which together form about a quarter of the population. The leadership of these churches speaks in a very positive way about this model. Vaguely, some allusions are sometimes made that there still exist some problems between state and church, but they hasten to add that these will be resolved. The situation is officially considered to be satisfactory and in their many international contacts Hungarian church representatives put this model forward as an example for those countries in the Third World that have opted for Marxist socialism.

The communist party in Hungary, too, sees itself as the exclusive guide on the way to a better future. It assumes that there exists a broad consensus between the leading party, which knows the goals of history and determines the way to attain them, and the people. Where this consensus does not seem to exist, everything should be done to attain it. The secretary of the State Office for Church Affairs, Imre Miklós said:

"We want welfare for the whole people, Our program is known to everybody. The majority of the workers agree with it, the population agrees with it. The believers also support our program. To cooperate does not mean to play the game of the communist party, as some would allege, but to put the program into action. We do not want to build society without the collaboration of the believers. Therefore our only desire is that the church helps us. There is a program of the Patriotic Front and clergymen were engaged in drawing it up. Atheists and believers together have voted on it at the congress... Therefore, our purpose is to realize the program. This is all we desire. The church must be able to live in peace and do its work. The believers should not live in a constant tension. If they do not, people will be able to work better(8)."

The ideological character of society is not accentuated here; all emphasis is put on pragmatic cooperation. But it goes without saying that the party determines the aim and content of the policy. "We declare," continued Miklos, "that we are a Marxist state, but that does not mean that everybody who lives in it is a

Marxist." The Hungarian regime takes into account that there are churches and Christians who are no adepts of the official ideology, but that does not mean that these can make an independent contribution or can take an independent stance in regard to government policies. Vice-premier György Aczel said:

"Marxism-Leninism exerts the ideological hegemony, because this is a scientific ideology which, according to its essence, can disclose the deepest problems of our time and can give the best anwers to it."(9)

The church must not only renounce the idea of a dialogue about the principles of Marxism-Leninism, but cannot put forward its own social principles. The communist regime assumes: (1) that it should accept the fact that Christians and churches exist, (2) that historical evolution leads to an evergrowing influence of the scientific (i.e., Marxist-Leninist) worldview and the dissolution of the 'mystical veil of mist', a process that the government must further, knowing however that the final aim of a communist society lies in a far future, and (3) that cooperation with Christians in the realization of the revolutionary aims of socialism is possible and useful if they are loyal and accept socialism as the program of the people.

The party shows the way and wants the support of the broad masses of the population. Thereby the churches can play an important role and the party expects the collaboration of leading church people in its politics. The church should not take a neutral position and those who want to stay aside risk being regarded as a silent opposition. And one of the most remarkable features of a communist society is that there is no room for even a silent opposition. The Hungarian regime wishes a positive stance of the churches and does not expect any criticism from that side, which it would immediately qualify as opposition. The Hungarian Protestant church leaders, in accordance with these expectations, pronounce themselves to be supporters of the socialist regime; they want to be 'a servant church' in socialism which accepts the social and political program of Marxism, with the exception of its atheist principles. They have developed a theology of service (theology of diaconia) and the synod of the Hungarian Reformed Church in 1960 pronounced its 'yes' to socialism:

"We hail the socialist edification and we offer anew for the final realization of socialism our prayers... In the forms of life of the new Hungary we discover the God-willed framework of a more just and happy Hungarian life."(10)

These churches have identified themselves to a large extent with the regime. They recognize that in principle churches have a prophetic-critical function in society, but for them this is the case for churches mainly in the Christian-capitalistic countries. In socialism the prophetic function of the church is not a critical function; in these countries it means that the church should give such an orientation to the people of God that it is willing to cooperate in the building up of a new socialist society. The prophecy of the church must recognize where positives forces are at work and support these.

Lutheran Bishop Zoltán Káldy also said: "The church, therefore, has put itself at the side of socialist development and has said yes to socialism, because she can see that this society does not only talk about humanism but realizes it."(11). In that connection, it has been stated that,

> "the Hungarian churches are of the opinion that the way to the future, according to the laws of social development, leads to a socialist world order. They confess that they have found their place and their service in that socialist social order which, according to their experiences, has more promising possibilities for the solution of the great world problems"(12).

The Reformed Bishop Lajos Bakos said at a meeting of the Patriotic Front: "Socialism means the world of freedom, of justice, of equality, and of humanity"(13).

Not only is a critical attitude rejected, but the prophetic task of the church is reduced to an appeal to conformism to the new order. The churches regard the line which the party chose after 1956 and the way in which it wants to build its own Hungarian form of socialism as the only feasible possibility for the country and they do not expect any positive results from a confrontation with the regime. But the question must be asked whether their conception of the role of the church is not an impediment to exploratory action to find where the limits of the rather tolerant policy of the Hungarian regime with respect to cultural matters actually lies. Because this is its present position, the church cannot function as the protector of religious groups, such as the Peace Group for Dialogue, that wish to pursue a more critical and independent course. It must also be pointed out that not all ministers share the views of the leading bishops. Leading personages in the church can only be nominated under supervision of and in cooperation with the government, which undoubtedly has furthered their course of conformity.

The GDR Model

The GDR is in large majority a traditionally Protestant country. The Protestant churches are united in the Federation of Evangelical Churches in the GDR, officially founded in 1969. The GDR churches have been able, in comparison with their Hungarian sister churches, to go a very different way. There are some very evident historical reasons for this. The most important might be the fact that the 'Landeskirchen' (people's-churches) in the Soviet zone had been able to maintain their links with the churches in West Germany. Formally until 1969, but actually until the building of the Berlin Wall in 1961, GDR churches were full members of the Evangelical Church of Germany. This has given them a stronghold and support in their endeavors to find a place in the new regime which tried at first to apply the Soviet model of church-state relations and to confine the influence of the church to a cultic ghetto. The second reason is that in its confrontation with the new situation that arose as an outcome of the Second World War, the churches could profit from the experiences of the Confessing church in Nazi Germany and the theological heritage of the Confessing Synod of Barmen in 1934.

The Hungarian churches with their strong nationalistic traditions were much less prepared for the social, cultural and political revolution after 1945 and did not succeed in resisting the temptation of a new identification with the powers that be. They did not have a strong and inspiring theological tradition, in which they could have found their foothold and a basis for a more independent and autonomous position in the new situation. If the situation in the GDR differs from that in Hungary, one of the main reasons was certainly that the GDR churches reacted to the new regime in a very different way. In speaking about the GDR Model, we confine ourselves to the policy of the main Protestant churches as formulated by Synods and Bishops. There exist of course a number of responses to the situation which are quite different. Among church members there are those who are primarily interested in a spiritual migration from society and there also exists a rather vocal group of partisans of the present regime, especially among members of the CDU in the GDR.

The attitude of the Federation of Evangelical Churches (Bund) has been expressed in a very concise formula: We want to be a church within socialism, not over against socialism, not in favor of socialism, and not alongside socialism. They refused to follow those who called for assimilation, opposition, or retreat from society. They wanted to find a way to combine civic loyalty, social engagement, and the freedom of an autonomous attitude in regard to the problems of society. The synod of the Bund held in Eisenach (July 2-6, 1971) expressed this as follows:

"The eight churches of the Bund regard the GDR as their state and take it seriously. The churches have made it their duty to help Christians to find that place in their state where they can fulfill their co-responsibilities in such a manner as the witness and service of the Gospel demand from them. The churches themselves are prepared -on their own or in the fellowship of the Bund- to participate in the process of communication which the state has with its citizens about the forms of their common future. They are convinced that in this dialogue they can contribute something very essential to insight into what man and what the human society is and needs, because they are called to the witness and servive of the Gospel. A witnessing and serving community of churches in the GDR will be obliged to give a clear account of its position: in this thusly formed society, not alongside it, not over against it. It will have to maintain the freedom of witness and service. Because on the basis of its vocation it is only commited to Him who as the incarnate will of God came to us to save creation."(14)

This declaration of intent has not put an end to the long process of learning in which these churches are involved. They still struggle with the problem in what way it is possible to be a witnessing and serving community in the corpus socialisticum.

The communist regime from its side had to learn how to live and deal with a church that is not willing to be changed into a collective chorus of assent or a one-way channel of communication from the party to the people. It was only after the erection of the wall in 1961 that the process started that led from an attitude of confrontation and rejection to acceptance of the fact that one had to live as a Christian within socialism. Gradually it became clear that the GDR was not a provisory or provisional state and that they should not continue to cherish the frustrating idea that to live in the GDR was a tragic fate. The challenge to live in this situation had to be accepted and the catchword of the Bund became: loyalty but then critical loyalty, cooperation but then critical cooperation.
  "We have not become a silent church," said one of the bishops. "When we speak, however, we do not want confrontation -we do not use agressive, polemical and offending tones. We do not look for conflict, but neither do we evade it at all costs."(15)

In principle the communist regime does not appreciate it when the church keeps itself at a critical distance. It wants the church to become a partisan of the socialist order. The church is not asked to abandon its faith and confession, but it should choose for what is good -socialism- and reject what is bad -capitalism-. Christians may have their proper motivation, their 'eigen motivierte Parteinahme', as the secretary of the State Office for Church Affairs declared in 1982:

"We assume that the separation and independence of the churches of our Republic in respect to the churches of the Federal Republic and separation of church and state -which

51

means the noninterference of the state in the internal affairs of the church and the noninterference of the churches in the affairs of the state- are as much in the interest of us all and certainly in the well-understood self-interest of the churches when they take sides with peace, disarmament, and detente on the basis of their own motivation."(16)

This really means that the church should restrict itself to purely religious matters and should not deal with social questions that are exclusively the domain of the party. It is, however, asked to support the policies of the party on the basis of its own motivations.

We constantly meet with this sort of reasoning when the Marxists in the post-revolutionary situation of East European countries speak about cooperation with Christians in the building of a socialist society and about the realization of 'true humanism'. Christians may have their own motivations to join in this process, but they are not expected to bring in anything of their own as far as the content of the cooperation is concerned. Before starting the dialogue and the cooperation they have to leave all their own ideas and principles in the cloakroom. And it is precisely that that the GDR churches do not want. They do not wish to identify, even out of their own Christian motives, with the existing society and hail the policy of the ruling party as the only possible and only right way for the future.

Bishop A. Schönherr expressed as his conviction that to be a church within socialism meant full-fledged participation in society while retaining its full autonomy and its proper profile(17). This attitude is quite different from that of the Hungarian Bishop Tibor Bartha, who said: "For Christians who stand in the imitation of Christ the building of human social conditions is a categorical moral imperative, though on the basis of a different inspiration and motivation."(18). He does not want to hear about a critical distance in respect to the regime, but considers this historical period, in which the government wishes to serve the interest of the people by uniting all creative forces as an act of Divine Providence. Critical loyalty has here been exchanged for conformism, as desired by the party. Here it has been accepted that Christians only have their own particular motives to cooperate, but that they are not real partners with their own principles and insights about the human being and society.

The churches in the GDR have chosen the narrow path by rejecting on the one side a full identification with party aims and methods, but by refusing at the same time to play the role of an opposition party. A very delicate position, because political opposition is not tolerated and the subtleties of the difference between critical Christian witness and political opposition are not always very clear, not even for Christian groups in other parts of the world, let alone for communist governments. The churches do not want to be regarded as politically dissident movements but rather as churches with their own specific task in society. They decline to form on the basis of the Christian faith a sort of anti-ideology with a competitive vision of the ordering of society. But they also refuse to consider the ruling ideology as a doctrine of salvation which would have the right to mould the consciousness of the people and they reject the pretension that this ideology contains ultimate answers to the deepest problems of human beings and society. The Gospel liberates the human being and enables him or her to see the ideology in its limited significance and to continue to ask critical questions about how far it serves in theory and practice human life. If, however, the Marxist-Leninist ideology becomes absolute and a closed world-view, then a conflict is inevitable. In an article titled 'Salvation Today', Bishop W. Krusche wrote:

"The faith that in Christ alone is salvation, is a critical correction of all actual idolatry, of all endeavors to give a messianic content to an engagement for the people (and) to qualify humanistic programs and ideas as doctrines of salvation."(19).

To a certain extent this self-definition of the churches in regard to their position in a communist society has been officially accepted. The meeting of the representatives of the Bund with E. Honecker on March 6, 1978, seems to have resulted in a prudent acceptance of this kind of role of the church in society. Problems were to be solved in a spirit of tolerance and mutual understanding. The protocol of this meeting has been described subsequently as a document 'von konkordatsähnlichem Charakter'(20) (in other words, a quasi-concordat). The tensions between church and state have not disappeared since then and they are invitable between a state which has definite ideological conceptions about the place of the church in society and a church which is not willing to let itself be locked up in a cultic ghetto or to function as decoration of the facade of socialism. The church, as a room for freedom and fellowship, presents itself as a societas alia, a societas alternativa, and a societas contraria(21). The tensions that this involves are an essential aspect of the struggle for liberation which the GDR churches carry on. They are in a real spiritual sense a liberation movement, because they resist submission to human concepts of salvation and refuse to accept the totalitarian pretensions of the regime.

Relevance for the Ecumenical Movement

An East-European theologian declared in a WCC publication(22) that ecumenism in Eastern Europe is very fragile and that the state might encourage it to keep the churches away from their internal, local mission. The possibility of a free and autonomous organization is not possible and the state tries to use ecumenical church bodies for its own purposes.

It is remarkable, but after what has been said not surprising, that the Protestant churches of Hungary play a predominant role in the organization of a sort of COMECON-ecumene. The Reformed Bishop Karoly Toth succeeded Metropolitan Nikodim as president of the Christian Peace Conference (Prague) and since then the activities of this peace movement in the Third World have increased considerably. The Lutheran Bishop Káldy, one of the well known church diplomats, said in the report to his synod (Feb.1981)(23) that in a period of four years he participated in 160 conferences and meetings abroad "to make known our views and to strengthen interchurch relations;" he received at home 80 delegations from abroad. In a meeting of the National Peace Congress in 1973, he explained:

> "We support the foreign policy of our socialist state and we devote our international contacts to the furtherance of the peace endeavors... our primary peace work is our stand for socialism, out faithfulness to it, and the fortifying of this faithfulness. For us peace and socialism are indissolubly interrelated."(24)

His colleague, Bishop E. Ottlyk, observed that

> "Our churches raise their voice in the forums of world Christianity... This is a sign of the aspiration that the Christians of the world become a worldwide camp for the futherance of peace and the friendship of people."(25).

In the Hungarian Parliament, of which he is a member, Káldy remarked in 1976 that the excellent relations between church and state in Hungary bear fruit and are a stimulant for those countries in Africa which have chosen the socialist order. "We like to inform the churches in these countries about our experience and we exhort them to accept the new social order and serve positively in it."(26). In his report of 1979, he spoke about the new relations with the Lutheran Church in Ethiopia:

> "Our aim was to encourage the church which lives in a new revolutionary situation and to strengthen its insight that the building up of a socialist social order does not impede the service of the church."(27).

At a meeting of the All-African Conference of Churches, Bishop Tóth, as leader of a CPC delegation, stated that the CPC is always willing to help the churches and church organizations

to get more easy access to the socialist countries,(28) and
Professor E. Kocsis wrote in a CPC publication that the socialist
countries have become models of the development of the Third
World(29). He added: "The churches and Christians of the East
European countries have on the basis of the human aims of the new
society decided positively for socialism." These leading voices
continually emphasize that devotion to peace is preceded by a
choice for the existing Marxist socialist order. Peace work in
this sense is an aspect of the ideological and political
confrontation. Nowhere else do we find this so clearly expressed
as by these Hungarians.

It should not surprise us that it was the Hungarian Bishop T.
Bartha, together with the Lutheran General-Bishop Jan Michalko
from Slovakia, who took the initiative to approach the Moscow
Patriarchate with the request to organize a conference of WCC
member churches from socialist countries in 1974, with the aim
'to come to a common policy and an intensification of their
contribution to Christian unity, peace, and collaboration of
peoples."(30). This was the starting point for a number of such
conferences held since.
The GDR churches showed great reluctance to be inserted into
a sort of block of East European ecumenical churches. They do
resist the pressure to become vehicles of ideological and
nationalistic propaganda and to defend the interests of their
home state.

But the action of Russian and Hungarian churches in the
international field are rather vigorous and, generally speaking
fully in line with the political views of the Warsaw Pact
countries. Their motivations are different: the Orthodox churches
participate in peace work out of a national-patriotic background,
Hungarians often seem to be inspired by their political stance in
favor of socialism. others do it on the basis of purely pragmatic
consideration, they simply have to do it and are too weak to
resist the pressure under which they live. All of them have at
the same time their purely churchly reasons: they need the
contact and the spiritual fellowship of their sister churches in
the West and they hope that their position in their own country
might be strengthened by their service to national political
aims, an expectation which unfortunately is scarcely realized in
practice. The bishops of most Roman Catholic churches have been
able in the main to adopt an aloof stance towards participation
in the communist peace actions.

In my opinion the peace work of a number of churches of
Eastern Europe is used by the state authorities for their own
purposes. If this testifies to a new and real social and
political engagement of the churches is very questionable. The
actions for peace of these churches are not just an expression of

a new self-consciousness of the believers, but instruments of ideological propaganda and manipulation of the goodwill of the people. Russian church representatives when abroad, for example, have to take into account legislation about slandering and descrediting the social system - a rather vague article which makes it a dangerous thing to utter any critical statements about the policies of their own country. There is no possibility for a free discussion of social and political issues in the parishes (except in the GDR and Poland) and they have no independent sources of information or study groups. Usually statements and declarations of church bodies are not different from those of state and party. Their biblical and theological motivations seem to have an ornamental function. Even a theological working-group of the Assembly of the Christian Peace conference in Prague in 1978 remarked that the theological motivations in the CPC are rather isolated from its political praxis. In the words of Max Stackhouse in the Christian Century (31): are the peace efforts of the Russian Orthodox Church 'simpy an extension of the party line in sacred phrases?' This does not mean that a real longing for peace does not exist in the Russian churches, but the government has not, just like our own governments, any need of diverging opinions about the way to attain peace. Contrary to our situation, however, the government of the Soviet Union uses all posibilities to suppress deviating ideas.

This captivity of the churches makes it difficult to come to close cooperation and to common ecumenical declarations about socio-political questions. In a consultation of the Conference of European Churches (CEC)(32) in which churches from the Eastern and Western parts of Europe collaborate, a Swiss theologian (H. Ruh, 1978) said:

"The churches have to devote themselves to the work for peace in their own sphere of influence. They cannot give a contribution to peace in the world by way of appeals across the border, but by way of changes in their own society. We must promise each other to do all we can in our own countries. Western churches are not served by appeals for disarmament from churches in Eastern Europe and these churches do not want such appeals from the West... Unfortunately the churches are often more willing to support changes in other societies...
Therefore they must be urged to take initiatives in their own countries in the interest of disarmament and peace."

Dr. Ruh asked the churches from Eastern Europe to take a more critical attitude in their own countries. Church actions in the West would be more effective if our churches could say: "Look at what our counterparts in the East are doing, they are also engaged in real work for peace and not just supporting party propaganda."

But unfortunately the situation is still such that most churches up till now, have not been able to attain an independent position in regard to the state. One of the few exceptions is the Council of Evangelical Churches in the GDR. The GDR churches have succeeded in keeping their internal autonomy and their actions for peace and peace education are critical also in regard to their own national politics. An Evangelical bishop of the GDR has, in a speech to a conference of the CEC, made a famous remark:

"Only those who fulfill their social duty in their own area, have the right to speak about what happens in the area of others. The churches can only serve peace if they not simply serve their own national interests and behave as amplifiers of the foreign policy of their own governments. If they only fulfill this role of amplifier, they loose their function as peacemakers. Churches which do not ask critical questions about the policy of their own government, but who declare this policy exclusively as peace policy are not the salt of the earth but the marmalade of their nation."(33)

This statement is extremely important, but it is unfortunately too easily forgotten. Most churches in Eastern Europe do not have the possibility to have an independent stance in regard to party policy and their peace work is outward directed. It is thus extremely difficult to come to common actions and declarations by these churches and the churches in the West, which usually approach the politics of their national government in a very critical way.

Salt and marmalade are not a pleasant mixture. Actions and declarations together with the churches of the communist countries (and again with some exceptions for the GDR) may even have a negative effect because they can raise the suspicion of being propagandistic and to be meant to undermine the position of one of the parties.

It is undoubtedly our task to maintain ecumenical relations with the churches in Eastern Europe but those who maintain these relations should be well informed about the real situation and not fall victim to ulterior propaganda intentions.

NOTES

1. 'Ein neues Interesse am Kirche und Religion. Kirche als Element einer socialistischen Nationalkultur?' Kirche im Sozialismus (KIS), 5/81, pp. 13-19
2. Ungarischer, Kirchlicher Pressedienst (UKP), 1981, pp.11-14
3. Nikolai Mizov, Voprosy filosofii (Moscow), no. 7. 1973, p. 77
4. August 8, 1980
5. No. 5. March 1980, pp. 45-55; quoted in Ost-Europe Archiv, 4/1980, pp. 191-198
6. Pressburgse Pravda, March 25, 1982, quoted in Informationsdienst. G2W, Vol.10, no.4-5/1982, p.13
7. June 1982, p.26
8. Orientierung. 45, no. 22, Nov. 30, 1981
9. Ungarischer Kirchlicher Pressedienst (UKP), 28, 1976, p. 23
10. UKP, 12, 1960, p.39
11. UKP, 26, 1974, p.4
12. UKP, 23, 1971, p.17
13. UKP, 28, 1979, p.20
14. See J.A. Hebly, Kerk in het socialisme, Baarn, 1979, p.68
15. Ibid, p.44
16. See P.J. Winters, 'Mehr als Irritationen', KIS, 2/81, p.24
17. P. Wensierski, 'Thesen zur Rolle der Kirchen in der DDR', KIS, 5/81, p.29
18. UKP, 29, Oct. 19, 1977, p. 20
19. Die Zeichen der Zeit. 5/73, pp. 172-181.
20. Otto Luchterhandt, Die Gegenwartslage der Evangelischen Kirche in der DDR. Tübingen, Mohr, 1982, p.56
21. Luchterhand, op, cit., p.105
22. Comment on Church-State Relations in Eastern Europe-Church and State, Faith and Order Paper no.85, WCC 1978, p.111
23. UKP, 1981, p.38
24. UKP, 1973, p.175
25. UKP, 1977, p.316
26. UKP, 1977, p.17
27. UKP, 1980, p.12
28. UKP, 1980, p.34
29. 'Christians and Churches in the Socialist Countries in the Struggle for Peace', in G. Bassarak, Christians Today in The Struggle for Peace and Social Justice, Prague, pp.120-128.
30. Stimme der Orthodoxie, 10/1974, pp.2-7.
31. 1983, p.584
32. Consultation Siofok 1978.
33. See J.A. Hebly, Kerk in het socialisme, 1979, p.86.

Chapter IV

THE CONSTRAINTS OF THE WORLD COUNCIL OF CHURCHES IN ITS RELATIONSHIP WITH THE CHURCH FROM THE SOVIET UNION

This essay deals with some of the questions raised by the participation of churches of the Soviet Union in the activities of the World Council of Churches: i.e. questions which are discussed more in circles outside the ecumenical fellowship than at ecumenical meetings. This is understandable when one realizes that, in such meetings, participants from Eastern Europe are also present.

It is rather embarrassing for those who have some sympathy for the predicament of representatives of churches in captivity and who favour both dialogue and fraternal relations with the Orthodox, to raise such issues in meetings where the illusion that the churches have equal possibilities is carefully maintained.

More disquieting is the fact that in the ecumenical churches in our part of the world the issue is equally neglected. It is often suggested that the problem of East-West relationships has taken up too much ecumenical attention and that nowadays there are more urgent questions for the world-ecumene, such as the North-South relationship. Without denying the urgency of this problem, it is necessary now to demonstrate that the problems connected with the East-West relationship affect some central issues in the life of the Council and cannot be neglected with impunity if it still wants its critical voice to be heard in the North-South dialogue. The churches should now discuss seriously the question of the form and content of their cooperation with churches living in political and ideological captivity. There is certainly a growing criticism of the present way in which this cooperation is realised. This criticism is often expressed by those who object to any social and political engagement on the part of churches or ecumenical organisations. But not only by them. In the churches themselves, the question is increasingly asked: Can the World Council continue to function as a common body for witness and service of churches from East and West as this was done during the last twenty years? Should there now be a reappraisal of the possibilities which such a council can have in the present circumstances?

This essay is intended as a contribution to this discussion. It certainly does not plead for a rupture of the relationship with the churches living in a marxist society. Its intention is to reshape these relations in such a way that they become more effective for the inner life of these churches and the strengthening of their real mission and service in the life of their people; and not for a further enslavement in a system which ultimately strives after their elimination.

59

An old question posed anew: what will be the impact of the
Russian Orthodox Church on the WCC?

When the Russian Orthodox Church joined the World Council of
Churches in 1961(1) the member churches reacted very positively.
For centuries, the Orthodox Churches and the churches of the
reformation had lived side by side in indifference, mutual
distrust and ignorance. Contacts had been sought, especially by
Lutherans and Anglicans; but, after the revolution, the Russian
church was completely isolated from all ecumenical developments.
So, after the Second World War, there was a certain eagerness to
draw the Russian church into the new Christian world fellowship.
The general feeling was one of joy and satisfaction that the
Church of Russia, the martyrchurch of the 20th century, which by
the grace of God and the endurance of the saints had survived
oppression and persecution, had been allowed to join the
ecumenical movement. This was regarded as a sign of a steady
amelioration of the church situation after the Stalinistic
period. There was a flowering of hope in the sixties: hope for
political disengagement, the end of the cold war, new
developments in the communist countries and the beginning of a
Marxist-Christian dialogue.

The prevailing optimism in ecumenical circles was not based
on a thorough knowledge of the actual situation. Gradually,
however, more became known: mainly through the flow of Samizdat
publications which reached the West during the course of the
sixties. Only then, in wider circles, did the question begin to
be asked about the implications of the entry of the Russian
Orthodox Church for the work of the World Council of Churches;
especially in the field of social and political problems. The
leaders of the World Council in those days can certainly not be
accused of naivité. They were conscious of the real situation and
of the difficulties which the participation of the Church in the
Soviet Union would imply for the ecumene. Not the confessional
but the possible political bearing of churches from the Soviet
Union on the work of the World Council posed a problem for them.
Ecumenical Christians had constantly objected to the
cold-war-mentality. Prof. Cadier wrote after the first
Nyborg-Conference in 1959 (the Russian church joined the
Conference of European Churches before it joined the WCC):

"The meeting of the European churches in Nyborg was of great
significance for us. Especially the participation of
theologians of the Orthodox Church of Russia and the
opportunity it gave to enter into conversation with them was
greeted with joy as a long expected event. We thank God for
the opportunity to take up contact with representatives of
other churches in Eastern Europe, for which there is
otherwise very seldom an opportunity."(2)

But questions still remained. As early as 1946, an observer of the ecumenical scene remarked (3):

"Like the American churches, the continental churches which suffered under the Nazis were also eager to speak out on social and political evils of the day; yet the ticklish position of the churches in Russia since the Russian Revolution would make them extremely wary of joining in any statement which critically considered the policy of the Soviet government along with policies of other governments."

In the first official conversations between delegates of the Russian Orthodox Church and the World Council of Churches in Utrecht in 1958, the question of the social and political witness of the church was one of the topics. During the fifth session on 'The common concern of the Churches for religious liberty' Nikolay replied to the question of Dr. Frey "if the Church could speak to the Government if the Government had violated peace, freedom or justice.": "that in a country where church and state were completely separated the conditions under which some of the principles of the Amsterdam statement had to be applied were different." "The separation of church and state, effected in 1917, had as basis the complete absence of interference by the state in the church and the church in the state. The church did not make declarations against Government policy or the anti-religious activities of the Communist Party. The Soviet Government was neutral, but the Party made propaganda." Visser 't Hooft said that "the position of the churches in the USSR differed from those of churches in the West and they could understand the situation, but the difficulties began when Russian Church leaders criticized the governments of other countries." Metropolitan Nikolay replied: "If the Russian Church criticized governments in other countries it was because it was convinced that it was right." "This ended the discussion."

In 1962, Paul B. Anderson, an American adviser of the World Council in Soviet affairs, wrote a memorandum for the ecumenical leadership in which he formulated a number of important questions, such as:

"In what ways may Communist principles, policies and procedures seek current application to the specific areas of activity of each WCC unit? The granting of exit visas and other facilities to Russian Orthodox Church representatives implies recognition by the Soviet Government of the large potential influence of the WCC on world affairs; from this it follows that the Soviet Government may seek in various ways to penetrate and influence the policies and actions of the WCC to conform to Soviet policies."

Have these penetrating questions, however, been taken seriously or has the experience of the last 25 years shown that they were unfounded? Is there ample proof in the practice of the World Council that its social and political witness has become more diversified and remained unaffected by political forces which have such a strong grip on part of its constituency? Has the moral authority of the World Council gained in momentum because it has proved to be really objective and unequivocal and has not been affected by the ideological struggle going on in the world?

In what follows, the impact which the collaboration with the churches from the Soviet Union might have had on the social and political activities of the World Council of Churches will be examined in detail. This seems to be a legitimate question: because nobody can imagine that the participation of churches living in such specific circumstances, after a long period of severe persecutions, would not have affected these activities. Not everything could possibly proceed in the usual way; and, as E. Schlink remarked in 1958, it could be advisable that the World Council of Churches will show a greater reserve in making political pronouncements after the accession of the Russian churches. It would have been a real sacrifice on the part of the other churches to prefer the fellowship with these churches above their already established pattern of behaviour. It seems, however, that such a sacrifice has not been deemed possible or necessary by the churches which had founded the World Council; and which had such high expectations of its possibilities. The continuing engagement in social and political problems has made it impossible that the participation of the churches from the Soviet Union could be pursued without the active involvement of the political authorities of that country. The consequence of which has been that these churches have become more closely linked with state-politics and have been more and more treated as useful organs of its foreign policy. It seems, too, that the member churches of the World Council of Churches have underestimated the influence which the Soviet delegates could exert on the activities or the choice of priorities of the Council. Because of the fact that serious study of and information on the position of the churches in the Soviet Union and other Eastern European countries has not been undertaken by the World Council of Churches since the sixties, and because of the fact that the study and information done in and by other member churches have not been diffused through the channels of the ecumene, this question of the impact of Soviet churches on the activities of the Council has remained outside the ecumenical discussion.

It is not the intention here to come to final conclusions, but, rather, to raise some fundamental and important questions which cannot be neglected because they are in the minds of many ecumenically orientated Christians. The theological dialogue on faith and order issues between Protestantism and Orthodoxy falls outside the scope of this essay: as does the discussion about the ecclesiological meaning which the Orthodox Churches attach to this universal fellowship of churches. It may, however, be useful to point out that the Orthodox, in general, have more inner reservations about an ecumenical fellowship of churches than many Protestants. They seem to be less existentially involved in the life of the ecumenical fellowship than those Christians in the protestant churches who are ecumenically active. An observation which was also made by a number of delegates at the Vancouver Assembly, for instance, in regard to the participation of the Russian delegates in the groupdiscussions. This reservation has been clearly expressed by Metropolitan Nikodim in a scholarly address in Uppsala(4),

"The Russian Orthodox Church," he said "was invited to join the World Council by the love of brethren who feel how baneful are the divisions between Christians and by the awareness of the importance of co-ordinating the efforts of all Christians in their witness and service to men...
It would, however, be more exact not to speak of the Russian Orthodox Church 'joining' the World Council of Churches, still less 'being admitted' to the World Council of Churches, but rather of an agreement between the leaders of the Russian Orthodox Church and those of the World Council of Churches for representatives of the Russian Orthodox Church to enter into permanent collaboration with representatives of other Churches belonging to an association called the World Council of Churches. The Assembly held at New Delhi in 1961 gave its consent to a collaboration of this kind."

This interpretation of the collaboration of church leaders makes it clear that in the life of local parishes, ecumenical influence is still very restricted. The Orthodox Churches urged some strong objections in the Central Committee in Geneva 1976 against direct contact between the World Council and local parishes. Nothing which does not proceed from the hierarchy of the Church can be taken up in the life of the Church. The absolute embargo on all information from the West enables church leaders to allow only what they themselves judge useful to filter through into the life of the Church. But there are other factors which we have to take into account when discussing the position of Russian churches in the ecumenical movement, and which prevent delegates from the Soviet Union from functioning in the ecumenical fellowship in a way which is comparable with that of participants from Western countries.

These impediments can now be presented under three headings. In the first place, there are the psychological difficulties. The present generation of Soviet churchmen has been formed in a cultural climate where free discussion, personal initiative and a broad international orientation are not very prominent. An extreme form of Soviet patriotism, a climate closed to influences from abroad, a lack of information and an all-pervasive ideological worldview characterize the educational system. In the second place, there are the legal difficulties encountered by Soviet representatives when functioning abroad. They cannot function as free representatives of their churches; but are subjected to a legal code in which rather vague articles are formulated about slandering the Soviet Union and defaming the socialist system. These can be interpreted in such a way that any form of criticism or even keeping silent when critical views are expressed by others, can lead to prosecution. It is very difficult for a Western observer to measure the strain which this puts upon Soviet representatives. It demands a form of system-conformism which is unimaginable to a Western protestant and represses any form of spontaneity. Even personal contacts remain in the shadow of the state, which keeps a watchful eye on its citizens, wherever they may be. Sometimes, we can notice that in ecumenical circles there is an understanding of this predicament. After a rather heated debate on repression and human rights violations, the Melbourne Conference on World Mission and Evangelism (1980) declared:

"Some countries and people we dare not identify for the simple reason that such a specific public identification by the conference may endanger the position -even the lives- of many of our brothers and sisters, some of whom are participating in this conference. We therefore confess our inability to be as prophetic as we ought to be as that may, in some instances, entail imposing martyrdom on our fellow believers in those countries, something we dare not do from a safe distance."(5)

It is a way of indicating the limited possibilities which some ecumenical delegates have to speak freely. Those from the Soviet Union and some other Eastern European countries seem to be tacitly included, as these countries are never mentioned when the issue of repression and violations of human rights is on the agenda. One might say that the Melbourne Conference declares in this statement that some delegates can be considered as hostages of the ruling party of their homelands to ensure that nothing is said or done which might be unacceptable to those who have them in their power: a disturbing fact which must have serious consequences for the work of an organization.

But, in the third place, we have to mention the ideological influence under which Soviet citizens are living and their obligation to conform to the official socio-political positions, even when representing their church in the ecumenical movement. The Soviet state has its own idea of what freedom means. It is only guaranteed by the Constitution when exercised 'in conformity with the interests of the working people, and in order to strengthen the socialist system.' Even those who claim not to be in agreement with the theoretical principles of Marxist-Leninism are placed under an obligation to cooperate in the building up of the socialist system and to serve its interests. Church representatives are not exempt from this obligation. To what extent this influences and determines their participation in the ecumenical movement will have to be analyzed later.

Soviet ideologists and the World Council of Churches

In his book Sovremennyj Ekumenizm(6), the author, N.S. Gordienko, describes and analyses the ecumenical movement in order to be better equipped for the ideological struggle against religion and the neutralizing of ecumenical influences on Soviet people. According to his view, the ecumenical movement has arisen in capitalist society and is still very much influenced by bourgeois ideology. Church circles, alarmed by increasing secularization, wanted to overcome the crisis in the life of the churches and consolidate the strength of the churches by seeking unity. The link of the ecumene with imperialistic forces which want to profit from inter-church collaboration is very clear. The present protagonists of anti-communism regard ecumenical unity as a force which can slow down the process of revolutionary change in the world and oppose the spreading of the ideas of scientific socialism among the masses. The World Council of Churches wants to stand above the classes and the parties; but behind it stand the interests of the exploiting classes of bourgeois-society. The churches wish to defend ideologically the capitalist world, whose spiritual product they are. The author, however, notices some changes through the influence of the churches from the socialist and the developing countries. It has now become much more difficult to exploit ecumenism as an apology for capitalism and for the discrediting of socialism. But there is still, after all, a pro-imperialistic orientation; and neutrality is cast aside as soon as there is a sharpening of the class-struggle: as became clear for instance, in 1968 during the events in Prague.

By joining the ecumenical movement, the churches from the socialist countries wanted to strenthen their position in their own societies; and, at the same time, to utilize the possibility to make known the points of view of believing citizens from socialist countries about social-political and religious life. They wanted, moreover, to give objective information about the position of religion in socialist countries and to unmask bourgeois-propaganda about the persecution of the church in socialism. The actions of reactionary forces were being condemned by the representatives of the churches in the socialist countries and the peace-forces in the World Council of Churches were strengthened by their participation. These church-representatives regarded Western social concepts as tendentious and unacceptable for citizens from socialist countries. They rejected bourgeois social ideals and affirmed against these their analysis of the inexplorable process of social development.

Not so much on the basis of theological arguments as well as on the bases of the factual existence of two mutually exclusive socio-political systems, they indicated that in the front ranks of social progress there is no more room for capitalism with its polarisation in the richness of a few and the poverty of the majority, with its exploitation of man by man, with its exclusion of the workers from the government of society, with its crises and unemployment, colonialism and racial discrimination, the influence of monopolies and the rule of militarism, but socialism that brings to humanity the deliverance of all these social evils and that provides for every human being the optimal conditions for bodily and spiritual perfection (126). It has also been suggested that the ideas of people's property, general equality and the fraternity of all peoples have Christian origins and that for that reason the social ideals of communism are closer to Christianity than those of the bourgeois.

According to Gordienko, the World Council of Churches is fundamentally an instrument of Western political interest groups. The entry of churches from socialist countries is therefore seen as a possibility to make heard the voice of the citizens from socialist countries and to allign the World Council with the really progressive peace-forces. This has not, up till now, been totally successful; for those theologians who speak with the voice of the exploiting classes still call the tune. The author deems the collaboration of marxists and believers in the struggle against militarism, racism and colonialism to be possible; but there can be no dialogue in which they should mutually influence each other. The communists assume that Christianity offers no solution to the problem of building up society and of liberation from injustice and they continue to fight against the religious ideology, albeit with ideal methods.

Collaboration does indeed, in his view, imply that the communists define the aims and content of this collaboration. He rejects the idea that the World Council could take up a neutral position between communism and capitalism -to balance between these two systems has proved to be a fiction.

It is interesting to note that this atheistic author stresses the protestant predominance in the World Council. According to him, there is no equal representation for the Orthodox Churches, and the staff has mainly remained protestant. The position of Orthodoxy is, however, gradually improving. The Soviet-author

seems to interpret 'protestant' as 'western' and his final
conclusion is that, in view of the continuing sharpening of the
class-struggle in the capitalist world and the convincing
demonstration of the perfection of socialism by the socialist
countries, the most important mission of the ecumene in the eyes
of the Western churches is to support the capitalist system and
to discredit socialism and communism. The fulfillment of this
task is being hampered by the presence of religious workers and
organisations which support the interests of the Christian
workers. The predominant position of bourgeois-Christian leaders
(these will be protestants in the eyes of the author) assures,
however, the former pro-imperialistic orientation.
For Gordienko, the World Council is, therefore, not a forum in
which the churches try to find in common counsel their own answer
to social and political questions, where they try to develop
their own vision and their own values. On the contrary, it is an
arena where Western-capitalist and Eastern-communist ideas
confront each other and collide. The duty of the representatives
of the churches in the socialist countries is, according to this
party-ideologist, to fight what he regards as reactionary forces
in the ecumene, to represent socialist positions and to blunt
anti-communist tendencies. They have not yet succeeded, however,
in obtaining such an influence in the World Council that it
adopts really progressive aims and principles. Western
conceptions, presented as generally humanistic or Christian,
still dominate.

The Handbook of Atheism (7) clearly states that religion, in a
class-society, is always at the service of the ruling class and
that, in our time, the bond between the religious organisations
with bourgeois-governments has become closer than ever. In a
post-revolutionary society, on the contrary, the church has,
because of the separation of church and state, been freed for its
proper task: which is the satisfaction of religious needs. The
state does not interfere in the religious activities of the
believers and their organisations; and these do not interfere in
the affairs of the state and of the society. Ultimately, religion
will totally disappear because it no longer has any real social
function.

It is clear that Marxist ideologists, who have a very narrow
conception of the real task of the church and reject any
interference of the church in the life of society, cannot make
any allowance for a social or political mission of an
international church-body in respect to their society. In their
view, there is no room at all for an independent international
council of churches which could pretend to stand above the
antagonistic social systems and would be able to speak about both
of them from an objective Christian point of view. A World
Council of Churches, in which churches from the

bourgeois-capitalistic society and from the Marxist-Leninist society collaborate, and are trying to find an independent common Christian position on social-political problems, is an anomaly for Marxist ideologists. There is no common task for the churches living either in a pre or in a post-revolutionary society. The church, in a pre-revolutionary society belongs to the super-structure of a class-society and is a reflection and instrument of, sometimes even protest against, such an exploitative, suppressive society. Only the church in a post-revolutionary society is free for its real task: the satisfaction of the religious needs of those citizens who still want this.

It is unimaginable that churches living in such totally contradictory conditions should have a common mission or could be able to formulate a non-partisan, objective opinion on the affairs of the world. It is even more unimaginable that an international church council should be allowed to raise a prophetic-critical voice against injustices in the socialist part of the world. Any criticism of socialism, where the society is build up on the basis of justice and which develops in the direction of peace and justice, can only be interpreted as anti-communist action from the side of lackeys of oppressive capitalist governments.

From this ideological position, the participation of churches from socialist countries in an international church body can only be justified if these churches function in such a body as the defenders and protagonists of socialism and try to change it into an ally in the struggle for social revolution under the guidance of the motherland of socialism.

The book on Christian Ecumenism by Y.V. Kryanev (8) does not differ essentially from that of Gordienko. He also speaks about the concept of 'transcendence' of the church which he, rightly, regards as a characteristic of the World Council. With this concept, the World Council has tried to show that it can take up an independent political position and cannot be regarded as just a reflection of political interests. For a Marxist, however, this pretention is untenable. Kryanev ascertains that a reorientation is taking place through the influence of churches from the developing and the socialist countries, but the former influences still prevail:

"There are still endeavours to create an atmosphere of anti-communism and anti-sovietism. Reactonary churchleaders from Western countries, incited by imperialistic circles are continiously trying to play up the question of human rights with tendentious and falsified material."

His conclusion is:

"The dialectics of the ideological struggle obliges us to an uncompromising criticism of the religious ideas of ecumenism, many of which are just a variant of bourgeois ideology. But at the same time, it is necessary to support measures of the World Council of Churches and the actions of individual religious workers in the defence of détente and for peace, security of the nations, disarmament and social progress."

On the question of how it can be ideologically justified to collaborate in programmes of the World Council of Churches and with religious workers, an answer is given in an article in Pravda (16-11-1979), written by M. Mchedlov, Professor of Philosofical Sciences, under the title 'Problems of theory: religion in the present world.' It is interesting to note that even some years after the appearance of this article the attention of a foreign visitor at the office of the Moscow Patriarchate was especially drawn to this article, which his hosts thought very clarifying, important and helpful when trying to fathom the policy of the government. This may be astonishing for us, but we should bear in mind that the reflexions of the ideologists which are discussed here, are not just interesting, but nevertheless noncommittal expressions of individual scholars about the meaning of certain phenomena in the modern world, but, rather, the background and basis of the policy of the regime to which the churches also have to conform themselves willy nilly.

Mchedlov points out that the imperialists are using religion for their reactionary purposes in the defence of the capitalist system and the struggle against real socialism. But there are believing people and even some of the clergy who oppose this. There is a progressivity which can be dressed up in religious forms because of traditional influences. The progressive character of social movements should be recognized: even if traditionally believing masses bring into these movements their prejudices and weaknesses.
The Marxist-Leninist parties and the socialist countries should not restrict their contacts to a narrow group of 'chosen' revolutionaries, but cooperate with believers in the common struggle against imperialism, colonialism and reaction. The communists organise a many-sided cooperation with believing masses for the defence of the people, of democracy, socialist progress and the common action against monopolies and threats of war and facism, as was discussed at the communist congresses in Moscow (1969) and Berlin (1976). Mchedlov also raises the question of how the participation of religious organisations in socially progressive movements can be combined with the fundamentally conservative social function of religion. The explanation he gives is that no religious doctrine is capable of eliminating the aspirations of working people towards the affirmation of their human dignity and the improvement of their

conditions. The struggle for the economic and political interests of the masses is so important that religious motives relegate themselves to the second place if they collide with them. And, furthermore, the discontent of believers and their longing for liberation can, according to Marx's thesis, be dressed up in a wrong religious form under the influence of the traditions of the country and its religious development.

Marxist-Leninists deem a common activity of the workers, atheists and believers, in the service of the revolutionary renewal of the old world, to be both possible and necessary. The practice in the USSR, where for the first time in history real freedom of conscience has been realized, clearly demonstrates this. As the communists presume that social activity is closely related to the development of the social conscience of a person, they also help to liberate the believers from age-old errors and to develop their dialectic-materialistic world-view. But they do this by means of education and conviction. Communists do not act against believers but for them, to eliminate in their consciousness illusionary notions which hinder their allround development and spiritual maturity.

For Mchedlov the struggle against religion and the cooperation with believers can thus be combined.

The permission which the Soviet authorities have given to the churches to join the ecumenical movement must also be seen in the context of the cooperation of a broad front of believers and non-believers in the struggle against reaction and for social progress and peace. This has had some results 'for the ecumenical bodies cannot ignore the feelings of the believers in socialist countries' Yantsenko writes in the Journal of Science and Religion (9): "As citizens of the USSR the representatives of the Russian Orthodox Church defend in all ecumenical programmes the foreign policy of their state and urge an objective judgment of everything which is happening in the world." But he must also notice that they are very often in the opposition.

The Handbook for students at institutes of higher learning (10) states that the preponderance in the World Council of Churches of Western Christian leaders and organisations, which express the interests of the bourgeoisie and try to defend the principles of capitalism with the help of a united Christianity, gives the ecumenical movement a pro-imperialistic character and makes it into an instrument of bourgeois politics.

Resuming what has been said, we see that Soviet ideologists regard the ecumenical movement as a Western phenomenon, created to overcome the contemporary crisis in the Christian world, and to make the churches a more useful instrument of bourgeois politics and of anti-communist propaganda. This being so, the socialist world can feel fully justified in using, in turn, the possibilities, which this movement provides, for the furtherance of its own policies, interests and propaganda. The Marxist ideologists presume that the churches from the socialist countries try to propagate the views of the believing socialist citizens, who are evidently fully in accordance with the official views, to unmask the bourgeois propaganda about the persecution of the church in socialism, to propagate Marxist socialism as the solution of all social evils, to resist Western social ideas and to bring the churches and the churchmembers onto the side of the real progressive peace-forces. They strongly oppose the idea of a possible 'transcendence' of the World Council of Churches, with which they indicate the concept that this international body could develop independent social ideas and adopt an autonomous and neutral position in the social and political tensions which exist in the world. Neutrality in the class-struggle between socialism and capitalism is not feasible. It is, however, possible to support programmes of the World Council if these can be useful for a progressive, anti-capitalistic policy. The participation of religious workers from socialist countries in bodies such as the World Council finds a justification in the setting of the collaboration of communists with believers who adhere to progressive ideas. Soviet ideologists view the World Council of Churches as a suitable place to fight anti-Sovietism, to propagate Soviet-views and to unite the believers in the struggle for a new communist world-order. When they speak about a Western, protestant dominance in the World Council and complain that Orthodox Christians from socialist countries do not have the position which they should take up, we should not interpret this as a sign of their concern for equal confessional representation. They rather express with this complaint that Marxist-socialist views and ideas do not yet play the dominant role which such ideologists would like to see.

A hidden agenda

As said before, the writings of Soviet-ideologists are elaborations of certain themes under the direction of the party and can only contain the conceptions and guidelines which determine its official policy. The publications which have been analysed can therefore be regarded as official views which have a direct bearing on the ecumenical policy of the churches, through the channels of the Council for Religious Affairs which has the task to 'help' the churches in their foreign contacts. The churches cannot develop their own understanding of the task and mission of international ecumenical bodies independently from the ruling ideology, at least as far as social and political issues are concerned. But even about the role of the churches amidst competitive social systems, their task in society and the content of their prophetic preaching, they cannot freely decide.

71

The actual behaviour of the member churches from the Soviet-Union in regard to social and political questions is determined by the Council for Religious Affairs. The Russian Orthodox professor N.A. Zabolotsky, a member of the staff of the World Council of Churches, uses the Byzantine conception of the 'symphony' to characterize the relationship of church and state in the Soviet-Union (11)

"A 'symphony' which does not mean a 'compromise', but arises rather for the sympathies, inclinations and facts, from the whole existence of its members, who regard themselves as citizens of their Fatherland and behave in everything such as is typical for the members of Soviet society."

It is rather doubtful whether this historic orthodox understanding of the 'symphony' between church and state can meaningfully be applied to the present situation taking account of the separation between church and state, the atheist character of the state and the ideological concept according to which the ruling party anticipates the ultimate disappearance of religion.

But there are deeper implications. We must assume that the attitude of the representatives of Soviet Churches in the World Council of Churches is determined by a 'hidden agenda', dictated by the authorities. On this agenda there are not only subjects such as: the unmasking of critical voices as anti-Soviet propaganda, the presentation of Soviet laws on religion as completely acceptable and of the situation of the churches as satisfactory - it is one of the main duties of the Council for Religious Affairs according to its 1961 statutes to ensure that the churches actually fulfill this task. This 'hidden agenda' also contains such subjects as we saw mentioned in the publications of the ideologists. But these subjects are not theologically neutral; they impinge directly upon what has been described as the heart of the ecumenical movement.

In his address delivered at the Uppsala Assembly and printed in the Ecumenical Review (12) entitled 'The Russian Orthodox Church and the Ecumenical Movement', Metropolitan Nikodim said:

"In his report on 'The Transcendence of God' given in Crete, Dr. Blake also said that the Churches belonging to the World Council of Churches must always be ready to transcend the influence of their environment, which might limit or alter their judgment. 'The attempt to transcend all human limitations and the faith that God makes such transcendence possible is at the heart of the ecumenical movement' (Report of Central Committee, Crete, 1967, page 102, last sentence). Of course, everything must be spiritually discerned, especially the gifts of the Spirit of God (I Cor.2.14).

However, such an extreme spiritualization of the Church's thought, which endeavours to transcend all human limitation and to rise above all national and state interests, is not always in accordance with the will of God and with the true spirit of the Gospel, which reminds us to 'render to Caesar the things that are Caesar's and to God the things that are God's' (Matt.22.21). It is better to follow the plain, but sound advice of the Apostle: 'Test everything; hold fast what is good.' (I Thess.5.21)."

We have seen that this same concept of 'transcendence' was rather strongly attacked by Kryanev. Now Nikodim also opposes it, although he does not provide a strong theological basis for his argument. At least, the much misused text from Matthew 22, which we hear so often quoted by Russian churchmen, can hardly be regarded as an adequate basis for his refusal to take seriously the concept of 'transcendence'. Neither does he make it clear when the endeavours to rise above national and state interests are in accordance with the will of God and when they are not. It is true, of course, that Orthodox theologians and churchmen, traditionally, have a rather national, even ethnic view of the church and that the autocephalic principle has not furthered the supra-national character of the church. But is it orthodox shortcomings or ideological pressure which prevented Nikodim from understanding this conception of the transcendence of the church? There are orthodox believers who seem to have a better understanding of it.

In his letter to the 3rd Council of the Russian Orthodox Church Abroad in America, August 1974 (13) Aleksander I. Solzehnitsyn asked:
"How do we restore a Church that is not an offshoot of state administration, not subject to any (even the best) government authority and unconnected with any party? A Church in which the best projects of our unfullfilled reforms will flourish, directed as they were towards the restoration of the purity and freshness of originial Christianity?"

He referred in his letter to the age-old captivity of the Church to the powers that be. How we can restore the Church to its original independence? This question is essential not only for the Orthodox Churches in the Soviet Union or in exile but for all churches. There is not a single church which should not ask itself whether it has or has not succumbed to the temptation to serve two Lords and to daub the wall of human injustice with untempered mortar (Ezekiel 13:14), instead of being the salt of the earth.

In his book 'The Renewal of the Church' (14) W.A. Visser 't Hooft pleaded for the liberation of the Church which can and must live by the strength of the Word of God alone.

"In the modern world with its fierce ideological strife, statesmen and politicians seek constantly to use the Church for ends which are essentially different from the one and only purpose for which the Church exists. Many Churches are imprisoned in ideological fronts and exploited for secular goals without realizing what they are doing. But there is, thank God, another side to this story. Whatever the Marxists may say, the Church is not merely a product of its sociological environment. The Church which has been invaded by foreign forces can be liberated. When the Church realizes again that it is the creation of the Holy Spirit, that it lives 'by every word that proceeds from the mouth of God' (Matt. 4:4) and that 'the Word of God is not fettered' (II Tim.2.9) the great process of liberation sets in and the Church which had seemed to become a mere reflection of society or, as Karl Marx called it, nothing but the 'spiritual aroma of the world' emerges in its true and original character."

Visser 't Hooft does not specifically allude to the Church in the USSR, but in the ecumenical fellowship we must also interrogate this particular Church on these points.

In an article in Christianity and Crisis (15) the same Visser 't Hooft has also written:
"We believe in the Lordship of Christ and in the right of the church to proclaim the implications of this belief for relationships in a social or political community. We cannot give up this central conviction without giving up the very substance of the ecumenical movement. In this matter we cannot compromise with the Moscow Patriarchate or with any other church or government which denies the right of the church to exercise its prophetic ministry."

The rise of the ecumenical movement is closely linked with the idea that the churches could free themselves from national and ideological links and could find new possibilities for a prophetic witness. The Assembly of Amsterdam declared in the report of Section IV (16):

"Christianity cannot be equated with any of the economic and political systems. There are elements in all systems which we must condemn when they contravene the First Commandment, infringe basic human rights, and contain a potential threat to peace... We utterly oppose totalitarianism... similarly we oppose aggressive imperialism... The churches have a

responsibility to educate men to rise above the limitations of their national outlook... Christians must examine critically all actions of governments which increase tension or arouse misunderstanding... The churches should also support every effort to deal on a universal basis with the many specific questions of international concern which face mankind today...
The World Council of Churches should not weary in the effort to state the Christian inderstanding of the will of God and to promote its application to national and international policy."

Two basic principles had a prominent place in the ecumenical movement in regard to its mission in the sphere of international political life:

1. The first was that the Church, after having freed itself from its identification with political powers, can take up a 'neutral' position. That does not mean to stay out of the problems of the world or not to deal with political questions, but to come to an independent judgment. Thereby meeting and counsel of Christians and churches, which live in different social and political systems, play an essential role. International conferences and discussions are of fundamental value, provided they do not deteriorate into forums for propaganda. In such contexts they can try together to find new ways in the light of the Kingdom of God, they can test and interrogate each other in the willingness to be themselves corrected by the others. Out of this common reflection and after taking common counsel, an engagement in their own situation can follow.

2. The second basic principle was that there exist norms which ought to be accepted by all and have an objective value. "We find in official church statements, both international and national, clear-cut requirements which must be met if nations and peoples are to live together in a divided world." (O.F. Nolde). The WCC has always pleaded for the development of an international ethos (Uppsala) and the elaboration of generally valid norms. The emphasis on human rights must be seen in that light. No social or political system should apply these principles arbitrarily, or put them aside. The norm is always: what serves man and humanity. Social systems exist to serve men, not vice versa.

The ecumenical movement was from its very inception, a daring effort to lead the churches out of the slavery of national, political and ideological captivity. A liberation movement in the churches, away from the old links between throne and altar and from conformism to society.

Both these principles are in sharp contrast with the views of Marxist ideologists as discussed above. They decline to accept

75

the idea that an international church body could take up an independent position between the two contrasting socio-political systems which dominate the world.
The churches have to take the side of justice, that is of socialism, they should become partisans of the oppressed in the international class-struggle between oppressors and oppressed, they should support the progressive forces. By allying oneself with these progressive forces one is acting objectively.

That which has been called 'a central conviction' of the ecumenical movement in the first period is not only rejected by Marxist ideologists, but is also attacked by representatives of member churches from socialist countries. Nikodim questioned what has been called the 'transcendence' of the church and he could possibly find theological legitimation for this in the orthodox tradition. But he is not the only one; and he gets support from unexpected quarters; namely from a reformed bishop, the Hungarian theologian K. Toth, the President of the Christian Peace Conference, who plays an important role in the ecumenical movement. In a lecture in Debreczen (1976) he defended the thesis that the church should ally itself with those forces which determine history and support justice and progress. He calls it a temptation for Christians when they try to find a specific Christian position in the great conflict between the old and the new. A policy of independence usually serves the mighty and the status-quo. He also denies that the Christian faith can have a critical function. When Christians want to criticize both sides and say 'if capitalism is criticized then socialism should be criticized too.', we must be very careful. If the Christian faith pretends to find fault in the old and in the new, it then puts them both on the same level; and then, it hinders the forces which can bring change and conforms itself to the existing order. The struggle between capitalism and socialism, i.e. communism, is in his eyes a struggle between 'the old' and 'the new'. He chooses for the Marxist conception of historical determinism. The new era has come and the church should support communism. We could give other examples of East European theologians who reject this concept of independence or neutrality. Their presuppositions are the following:

1. The church should not pretend that it can take up an independent stance. According to Marxist ideas it is an instrument of the ruling classes and it is only liberated from this captivity in communism where the state does not need the church and does not use it to justify its actions.
2. One should not assume that on the basis of an international set of rules or formulated human rights, of objective or 'evangelical' norms, alienating tendencies in different social systems could be criticised.

Objectivity in this sense is not possible, according to
Marxist views.
3. Relativising of ideological systems is not possible,
because this would imply that people are not making a
decision in favour of the realisation of justice.
4. There is an almost apocalytic confrontation between the
two blocks, between light and darkness. Nobody can remain
aloof. The only possibility is to choose for the light and
the new against the darkness and the old. A third way does
not exist.
Here, the churches are admonished to declare themselves in
solidarity with the socialist block, because this leads the way
to the future. Socialism is justice, peace, liberty, progress,
the future: and one should say 'yes' to it.
A prophetic critical task of the WCC towards East and West
alike is not feasible in Toth's view. He is thereby fully in
accordance with the ideas repeatedly expressed by the Hungarian
member churches in the ecumenical discussion. It seems right to
have a closer look at them, in order to obtain a better
understanding of their ideas of the prophetic task of the
churches.

A short account of the prophetic task of the church as seen by
the Hungarian Reformed Church

The reformed churches realize that they have a prophetic task
and are called to proclaim the Word of God in the actuality of a
given historical context. But that is not an easy task and this
prophetic mission has become a central problem, as is said in a
publication of the Reformed Synod on the occation of the fourth
centennary of the Synod of Debreczen 1967 (17).

"In the course of the great social revolution which our
people has experienced in the last 20 years, our church has
never renounced to fulfil the service of the good Samaritan
and its prophetic ministry. The right biblical understanding
of this prophetic service and its practical evangelical
application has become a central problem of our church."

The Hungarian churches have issued a number of publications about
the theological questions connected with the prophetic service of
the church and how they can fulfil this in the present
circumstances. Their practice is to issue study papers prepared
by their Ecumenical Council for the main conferences of the World
Council of Churches, where they deal with the biblical
foundations of the prophetic service and the interpretation
presently given to it in Hungarian theological thinking. This is
done most elaborately in a study paper for the Uppsala Assembly
in 1968. The biblical validity of a prophetic critical attitude
of the church with respect to government and society is

recognized; but the present reality of the socialist society in which the church is living gives this prophetic-critical mission a specific dimension. In the first place, the church should not pretend to be the sole guardian of truth and as such to be able to sit in the judgement-seat. In the new order of society, the church itself stands under judgement: and has constantly to expiate its own sins and failures in the past. The main emphasis is put on this. The prophetic task means that the church proclaims the gospel, recognizes righteousness everywhere and associates itself with those who serve the good and do the righteousness.

The prophetic service is not negative-critical, as according to this document churches all over the world are presuming, but is meant to proclaim a new order which is in accordance with the will of God, to show what the way of God is in completely new situations, thus to avoid the danger to act against God's will. We than read (18):

"Here and abroad there were many of those who had expected from our churches a judgement on the new society, a critique under the pretext of the prophetic task. They underlined with special emphasis that the church has the right to qualify the changes in society on the basis of the eternal ethical norms of which it disposes and equally to draw the attention of the state to its failures. This claim contains two serious mistakes. Firstly because in its demand for criticism it only refers to the example of the prophets of the Old Testament who sharply condemned the kings of Israel. We have already, in speaking about the New Testament, drawn attention to the fact that one should never consider the prophet of Israel on his own, apart from the fulfilment completed by Christ. Secondly because the prophets of the Old Testament were prophets of the same Convenant people, whose theocratic rulers were reminded of the laws of Jahwe, laws accepted by the kings of Israel themselves.
In our situation we have not to deal with a theocratic ruler, but with a secular state, to which one cannot simply apply the norms of the prophetic word of the Old Testament, even though it is subjected to the general laws of humanity. Furthermore the call for a one-sided criticism is wrong because the church would then have withdrawn itself from its responsibility for the new society and have failed in its prophetic task."

It is said in another study document (19) that it is the prophetic task of the church to point to sin, injustice, exploitation and inhuman behaviour especially in 'Christian' societies. Furthermore, it should test which forces and movements are agreable to God and which are not and where the will of God

78

in regard to human relations and social justice is more fully obeyed. The church should point to injustice in Christian -i.e. capitalistic- societies and as Toth already remarked, should not put capitalism and socialism on the same level. The prophetic task of the church in socialism is to give such an orientation to the believers that they recognize where the good, the will of God, is done and become willing to participate in the building up of a new society. The churches have to side with socialism and

> "The Hungarian churches recognize that the way of the future leads to a socialist world-order, according to the laws of social developments. They confess that they have found their place and their service in this socialist society..." (20)

According to this point of view, the Hungarian theologians seem to adopt as their starting point the premisses that according to historical-materialism, and "not so much on the basis of theological arguments" as Gordienko rightly remarked, Marxist-socialism may be equated with the good, the future, justice and that the church has to choose for Marxist-socialism. How could it do otherwise than to choose for the good! It is evident that their attitude in the ecumenical fellowship of the World Council of Churches has been determined by this presupposition.

The hermeneutical key

The main problem in the ecumenical discussion is not so much the language problem, as the understanding of the meaning which lies behind the words and concepts used in the discussion. Basic to this essay is the suggestion that for a correct understanding of the contributions for instance from the Orthodox Churches from the Soviet Union, it is not simply necessary to know their specific traditional Orthodox theological background, to take account of a certain isolation from Western historical, spiritual and cultural developments and of their weak and threatened position in society. It is also just as necessary to take into account the limitations of their freedom to develop their own social and political thoughts and their obligation to conform to the official social and political concepts of the ruling communist party. This lack of freedom and this conformism -which is obligatory for those who act as spokesmen for the churches at home and abroad, even if some of them might not necessarily be personally in favour of the official concepts- are the hermeneutical key to the understanding of the position and contribution of these churchmen in the ecumenical discussion. Prof. J. Hromadka remarked at the Lund-conference (1952) (21) that in the ecumenical discussion we must be aware of hidden motives behind our theological reasonings.

"No matter how sincerely and confidently we assert that our problems are being viewed by us solely in the theological and biblical aspects, another motive force may be hidden in the depths of our spiritual life and our theological thought. Our efforts to understand the Word of God, may be changed in the most dangerous manner -unconsciously or almost consciously- by our apprehensions and our wishes in the social, political and cultural spheres."

With this warning in mind, it would be advisable in this respect to analyse, for instance, an article by prof. N.A. Zabolotsky, entitled: 'The society of the future: Justice, Participation and Sustainability'. (22) There are not many publications from the Russian Orthodox Church in the Soviet Union on social issues, apart from those which deal with the issues of peace, and Zabolotsky is one of the few theologians specialized in this field. The article deals with 'facts and phenomena' not only from a 'horizontal perspective' but tries to see the horizontal 'in the light of the vertical'. "When we speak of horizontal service for justice, we must not forget the vertical aspect," and so we find in the text a number of theological passages, loosely connected with the rest, "which bring to the world view the penetrating spiritual reality of the Godhead, which can only be understood through faith and love." But these specific theological thoughts are 'an obligation and the motive force only for Christians... (and) cannot and must not infringe upon freedom of thought and affairs of those outside the Church."

These passages seem to be meant to demonstrate that Christians have their own motivations and "hear the summoning Voice of God and the voice of the conscience of men of good will inside the Church and outside of her and are obedient to them both." What "obedience to men of good will outside the church" really means, is not explained. Usually these "men of good will" are identified with those who work for peace and justice along the lines of the communist party of the Soviet Union.

The article takes its starting-point in the WCC Conference 'Faith, Science and the Future' (Boston, 1979)
"A stimulus to this conference was the pessimistic view of the West with regard to science and technology, where the uncontrollable use made of them in so-called 'liberal' societies could have harmful consequences... In addition to this, the appeal of the socialist society, with its optimistic views of the future, constituted a fairly weighty argument in favour of holding the conference."

One of the underlying premisses of Zabolotsky's article is becoming clear right at the beginning. There are two main social systems, the socialist and the Western, and in this last system all the evils of the world seem to be concentrated, while on the socialist countries he only gives positive evaluations.

Some examples: Exploitation and impoverishment, also of the Third World, are 'the West's social problem' and justify the class struggle in developed capitalist countries and the liberation movements, but also the programme of the WCC. Concrete action is required to promote freedom from oppression as well as 'structural change in most societies today, where injustice is causing suffering.' There is the injustice with regard to the environment, but evidently not in the Soviet Union 'because the programmes of the Soviet Union are incorporated into the Constitution and implemented in practice.'
The two last centuries have been characterised by changes for the worst in all fields of life, but
> "Socialist countries, particularly the Soviet Union tried to break out of this vicious circle... In this complexity the countries of the Third World are trying to find their own way, looking both at the old order and at the new. Some of them have found the correct path to socialism."

Then Zabolotsky calls on everyone
> "to participate in the construction of a new world -a world of justice and a fuller and more perfect life. Man is a labourer together with God (I Cor. 3:9), which also means that he participates in the creation of this new world."

The author is using in this article a prudent and more modest language in his praise of socialism and the Soviet Union than in his article quoted above (23). But the intention is clear: socialism is the new order and labouring together with God means cooperating in the building up of socialism and in the class-struggle in capitalism. There is, as it is said right at the beginning of his article, no convergence of the dissimilar contradictory ideological systems and the ecumenical discussion should not try to find some general unified scheme which can lead to some comprehensive rapid convergence. Nowhere is indicated that there could be a task for a World Council of Churches in respect to the socialist system other than cooperating with it. Its task is restricted to the system "where injustice is causing suffering". There it has to promote concrete action for structural change to promote freedom from oppression, exploitation, racial discrimination.

The key to the understanding of Zabolotsky's article, which is written in a way which often obscures the issues rather than clarifying them, must be sought in the publications by the ideologists, analysed above.

A new methodology

It seems to be not unjust to draw the conclusion that influential participants from churches in Eastern Europe are convinced that it is their duty to use the influence they have not only to prevent the World Council from criticizing the socialist system, but also to make it a partisan of the progressive forces in the world; that is to say to make it instrumental to the cause of Marxist-socialism.

This would not be a too tragic situation if it means that, in the international fellowship of churches, a real dialogue could arise between Christians with different social and political ideas, who are free to come to a common opinion and are eventually free to change their ideas. These partners in dialogue, however, are not free but either in a political or an ideological -sometimes both- captivity. They are not members of a pluralistic society, where one is able to choose between different opinions, but part of a 'monolith' (Zabolotsky (24)), where those who are allowed to go abroad and participate in international churchbodies have to speak with the same voice as the ruling party, with whose ideas about the ecumenical movement we have made acquaintance above. They are regarded as emissaries of a system which assumes that it is in possession of the truth and the exclusive knowledge of the way to a future of justice and peace. They can, of course, use and develop their own Christian and theological motivations and arguments as long as the conclusions are in line with what is expected from them.

Many Christians have had high expectations of the World Council of Churches. They have regarded it as a possibility to come in common study and dialogue, to a better and more profound insight into what would be the will of God for our days, to be liberated from a narrow nationalism, to come to an understanding of the social and political ideas of others, to elaborate a new conception of a responsable society, more just, participatory, sustainable and peaceful. But this implied, of course, that all participants would first of all meet as Christian men and women on the basis of a common faith and would on the basis of this common faith be prepared to engage in a mutual dialogue about the consequences which this faith has for their life in the world. But a real dialogue, which is more than a mere exchange of opinions and convictions, implies the willingness and the possibility of change. With missionaries who have to propagate and defend their fixed set of ideas one can talk: but not dialogue. The World Council of Churches was seen as a way to seek renewal, justice and reconciliation and to come to a common understanding of the practical implications of the Kingship of Christ. Not to criticize one or the other social political system was the main target, but to find a new social and political ethos and to engage themselves in the realisation of it. An ethos which would transcend national, social and ideological boundaries which held the churches and the Christians captive. Many ecumenical

Christians did consider this 'the central conviction of the ecumenical movement.'

But there has been a considerable change in ecumenical methodology since the seventies, which has led to the accentuating of social action over against reflection about ecumenical Christian social ethics. In a lecture, held in Bern (Switzerland) December 1983, Paul Abrecht has remarked that in the new ecumenical approach:

"Action means commitment to a cause, efforts to persuade the churches to support that cause and involvement with people and groups struggling for it."

The word 'solidarity' has in this connection become very popular. Christians must achieve solidarity with those who struggle for liberation, peace, justice and not deliberate about the theoretical aspects of our common obedience. Some people are of the opinion that it is not the main task of the churches to formulate 'abstract' ethical principles which should then be applied to concrete situations. But is it not necessary to come first of all to a common Christian understanding of what justice, peace, liberation means and which are the ways to work for it? And is there not the danger that people use the same word but give a totally different meaning to it?
This is actually happening in concrete actions and situations. Can a Christian, without asking questions about the underlying presuppositions, identify himself with any action for peace, even with those who identify peace with the establishment of Marxist socialism? For the churches in the GDR this is a burning issue and they try to find the theological and ethical criteria to which any common action for peace should correspond. If this is not done, secular and ideological categories will prevail.

In a WCC document (25), in which the Hungarian Reformed Church comments on the report of a WCC-commission 'Towards a church in solidarity with the poor' we even read a recommendation to take over ideological categories. It is written there:

"The theological basis of our churches can still be summed up as 'the theology of the Gospel', although we are in agreement with the new concepts of theology: revolution, liberation, development and peace, etc. However, we feel that when we try to liberate the poor, build the foundations of lasting peace and promote social justice and people's participation, it is a revolutionary ideology, not theology, which can serve the people."

A much more thorough semantic discussion needs to take place in the ecumenical movement about the meaning and content of words and concepts which are used. This becomes quite clear when reading such a passage. But there are other consequences of the change in ecumenical methodology, which has issued from accentuating the need for action and for the identification of the church with causes arising from concrete situations. This could easily lead to a selectivity which is detrimental to the position of the World Council of Churches. If those who propagate the idea that only in one part of the world is there injustice, oppression, exploitation etc. have a say in deciding what actions the church should solidarize with, it has proved to be quite easy to concentrate all activity on that part of the world. If, moreover, there is a situation in which only the churches from one part of the world can take the initiative to act in situations of injustice and try to get the World Council involved in their action, this selectivity is being strengthened.

Concretely, those who wish to solidarize with the cause of the aborigenes in Canada or Australia can easily try to get the World Council on their side with the consent of the churches involved in these causes. But who can bring officially the cause of Charta 77 in Czechoslovakia or that of the Crimean Tartars to the notice of the World Council and plead for solidarity with their struggle for greater justice?

This accent on social action seems to be rather convenient for those who are not able to participate freely in the reflexion on an ecumenical social ethos and who have to abstain from the working out of ecumenical Christian social concepts, which may not be in harmony with the secular ideology to which they are subjected, but transcend existing national, regional, political boundaries.

Cause-selection

It does not seem to be exaggerated or totally wrong to draw some conclusions: a number of member churches in the World Council of Churches are convinced or at least take the position

a. that in their part of the world justice and peace have already been established or at least are being realized by the government and that churches have no special task in or towards those countries. Prof. Zabolotsky (26) speaks about the 'normal' relations between church and society, as did Gordienko, which means that the Church can fulfill its specific task (liturgy, preaching, pastorate, theological education and research) without engaging in specific social and political activities;

b. that the struggle for a better society has to be pursued in the non-socialist part of the world and that the churches and the World Council of Churches can make a contribution to this struggle. Moreover, the churches should openly recognize that injustice has been overcome in socialist society and

collaborate with the progressive forces in the struggle for
more justice in the rest of the world.

In his report on Nairobi (27) Bishop Mikhail wrote about the work
of section II:
"We must ascertain that speaking about negative phenomena in
the world -unjust distribution of material goods,
exploitation, poverty, hunger, oppression, illiteracy- the
document orientates itself almost exclusively towards the
capitalist countries and partly towards the Third World. It
leaves aside the rich experiences of the socialist countries;
experiences which, as is well-known, were acquired in the
struggle against these evils until their radical removal.
Accordingly, the descriptive part of the report and the
recommendations suffer from the usual onesidedness and
shortcomings."
The Bishop seems to understand by onesidedness and shortcomings
the fact that the evils of the capitalist world are mentioned
without at the same time mentioning the good, the abolition of
these evils, in the socialist world.

For a number of member churches the slogan of the World Council
should not be 'the world is my parish', but 'the non-socialist
world is my parish'. This is not meant as a malicious attack on
the world fellowship of churches, but as a statement of fact. A
fact which seems to be almost inherent to any religious world
organisation in which orthodox or protestant churches from
Eastern Europe are active members.

In July 1984, the Lutheran World Federation held its Assembly in
Budapest, Hungary. Günther Krusche (28), a GDR theologian,
remarked in an interview after the Conference that: "Although
this conference was held in a socialist country it did not bring
anything, which could have been important for this context."
Preceding the assembly a youth conference took place with 300
young church-members from 49 countries; among them 48 from the
GDR and 86 from East-European churches. Central topic of the
discussion: the situation in Southern Africa and the unjust
economic and social structures of oppression in the Third World.
In The Information Bulletin for Lutheran Minority Churches (ed.
Budapest 8/84) a participant from the GDR wrote about his
impressions under the title: 'Is Eastern Europe not a theme?'

"I cannot introduce a new social system in South-Africa or in
India, said a Polish delegate. He would rather have discussed
the situation of the young people in their own churches and
have heard about the experiences of others with evangelism
and biblestudy. But this was not discussed. Only a pastor
from the GDR spoke about 'peace and justice in an East-West

perspective', otherwise Eastern Europe would have been completely left out of the discussion."

In these words of a young East German Lutheran we have in a nutshell the present ecumenical situation. Eastern Europe is not a theme in the ecumene. Nobody can deny that advocacy for justice is an essential, integral part of the mission of the church and that the Christian faith demands action consistent with its commitment. It is equally true that the church cannot restrict itself to the intellectual formulations of general principles, but that it should give a living witness in solidarity and suffering. But what is true of the church in its social and historical context has not necessarily to be true of a world council of these churches. A continuous debate is going on in the ecumenical movement about the ecclesiological status of the World Council. It cannot, according to common opinion, be equated with a church. But usually no account is taken of this distinction between a church and a world council of churches when the task of the church in society is being discussed. But we should not only take into account the ecclesiological differences between a church and a world council of churches, but also have at the same time an open eye for the variety of political and ideological situations of the member-churches, which makes it impossible for a world council to act as a church for the world. It can and should discuss the role which the churches should play in the social sphere, but cannot play it itself.

In the present situation, a world council has only restricted possibilities, because as a 'world' council with a constituency which in part has no independent and autonomous position, it is not really free to decide to what cause it should commit itself. It is very true what Patriarch Pimen remarked, that there is no single, universal all-Christian answer possible to the themes with which the ecumene is dealing, because of the difference in circumstances, cultures, economic and political systems (29).

A universal council should therefore be reticient to identify itself with the concerns of churches in local (i.e. national or regional) situations. A universal fellowship of churches should stimulate the churches to fulfil their mission in their own situation and it should discuss the overall-concepts and the theological-ethical guiding principles for the social action of the churches. These should then be translated and adapted to the different circumstances, because the form and content of the social action of the churches may be quite different. It might also provide a platform where churches, engaged in their local situation, can exchange experiences and eventually seek the help of the other local churches which are concerned with the same problems or feel committed to their cause.

But can a universal council solidarize with some local churches in such a way that it takes their special concerns and priorities as its own concerns and priorities? And, if it does, which factors play a rol in deciding which priorities to take and which local of regional causes to identify itself with? We have already mentioned a number of reasons. Some causes have strong defendants and promotors in the ecumenical bodies, while others cannot find sufficient support or are even vetoed by member churches. Some causes could have divisive consequences for the ecumenical organisation, while others are expected to have a unifying aspect for the life of the fellowship; which usually proves not to be the case. A certain selectivity with respect to 'causes' is necessary and inevitable for a world-organisation which wishes to engage in concrete action. But, if this selection, because of the attitude of a number of member churches based on ideological concepts incompatible with Christian principles, has as a result that one part of the world is always falling outside the scope of this world-organisation, a serious question arises. Is it a good policy for this world-organisation as such to engage in concrete action? Or should it encourage its member churches to discern the challenges put before them and to engage in these causes on a local or regional level? It could also be envisaged that some local churches become engaged in the concerns of other local churches and covenant together for a common cause in which they feel a common responsibility. But a concerted engagement in local causes by a universal body might, in the present circumstances, even be disadvantageous for those causes.

It might be advisable for the World Council of Churches to change its pattern of behaviour and to resist the pressure of those who want it to express itself on all sorts of actual problems in which they themselves are engaged. The procedure at the Assembly of Vancouver (1983) in respect to the Afghanistan and Middle-America resolutions has given rise to a number of commentaries. Probably the most interesting came from an East-German commentator in the journal 'Die Junge Kirche' (30), where he says:

> "The voice of the World Council of Churches must be consistent (einheitlich), recognizable as one and the same voice of this worldwide Christianity, guided by the same principles. When that is not possible it would do better to keep silent."

This quotation seems to summarize in a very concise way the thesis contained in this essay.

A tension exists in the ecumenical movement on the subject of the nature, function and possibilities of the World Council of Churches. Different views exist and collide. On the one hand, there is the opinion that ecumenical councils are a consultation-structure, where not only different confessional, but also socio-political points of view are in discussion with each other. The participants have pledged to take each other seriously and to listen to each other; but also to be open to mutual criticism on the basis of the commonly-accepted norms and values. The ecumene as a consultation-structure presupposes a specific spirituality and although not a product of Western-democratic origin (see Acts 15), it can certainly flourish in that soil. A certain common understanding of the aims and values is a neccessary pre-requisite if ever these consultations are to lead to action and not just remain an exchange of interesting opinions. These actions will usually be determined by a liberal-evolutionary way of thinking about the development of society. That this way of ecumenical cooperation cannot lead to actions, aimed at changes in social and political life and always tends to consolidate the status-quo, is an unjust and unrealistic reproach. But in the churches other ideas have come up, which are linked with a more radical-revolutionary concept of society. Councils of churches are then seen as action-structures, spear-heads of church activities in social and political life. The background is not inclusiveness, but partisanship, a radical choice for justice, the new, the future. Problems of society are reduced to the antithesis between two mutually exclusive positions.

This way of thinking seems to be influenced by the concept of the class-struggle, which starts from the assumption that there are clearly recognizable contrasting positions and that a Christian should and could make a clear choice. These different conceptions seem not to have become the subject of a real dialogue.

The price which the WCC has to pay for its silence on Eastern Europe

In speaking about the first years of the World Council of Churches W.A. Visser 't Hooft (31) remarks that the young ecumenical movement already had in those years a certain tradition in the area of social thought and action. Important elements of this tradition were: the common conviction that the churches should be concerned not only with the spiritual and moral life of individuals, but also with the problems of society; the quite substantial consensus of the content of the Christian social ethic; the method used to enable the churches to make their own specific contribution to the life of society. One of the elements of this method was to arrive at a definition of the fundamental issues with which the churches should be concerned in order to render their witness to society.

The problem which concerns us is how the identification of these fundamental issues is taking place.

Visser 't Hooft shows that delegates from Third World countries did raise urgent problems for study and discussion and that the awareness of the astounding achievements in the field of science and technology (genetics, nuclear power, ecology) posed a series of problems with which the churches ought to be confronted.

When one views the large range of issues with which the WCC has occupied itself it will be very difficult to prove that any of these has been brought into the ecumenical discussion by the Russian Orthodox Church or, for that matter, by any church living in the communist commonwealth of nations. The Russian Orthodox Church -a conservative church in a conservative state (32)- has not been able to develop a real involvement in the problems of society. The short period before 1917, when this church did discuss a social programme, came to an abrupt end with the establishment of the Soviet regime which marginalized the church, forbad any activity in the social field and did not even allow the study and discussion of social questions. The church has to confine itself to cultic matters only and accordingly has not been able to create a cadre of specialists in the field of Christian social ethics.

The Western and Third World churches are responsible for the agenda of the WCC and whatever radical or other influences, reprehensible in the eyes of critical Western observers, there might have been, issue from their representatives. "The source of the protest against the West is the West." (33)

Latin American theologians have played a rather prominent role in this process of identifying the issues of concern for the ecumene. They have pleaded for a profound transformation of existing socio-economic structures and have accused the Western democracies of maintaining a system of increasing exploitation through their multinational corporations. It must equally be said that the ecumenical churches in the USA were ahead of most of the other churches in their criticism of American policy (e.g. Vietnam or Middle-America).(34)

The ideological flavour of a WCC study-paper, strongly influenced by Latin-American theologians and received with some scepticism in Western circles, 'Towards a church in solidarity with the poor', was even criticised by the Russian theologian N.A. Zabolotsky (35). He says:

"It should definitely be stated that liberation theology and its particular conclusion -the theology of revolution- have ideological implications. Social, economic and political elements in this type of theology are in essence merely human reflections on world processes... But in such cases, there will inevitably be a clash both in ideas and in action between similar ideologized theologies and other ideological structures."

For a Russian Orthodox theologian, there should be no confusion between theology and ideology. That is one of the guiding principles in his church; but also in the party which dominates his country. The party takes the view that theology has to do with the supra-natural but should not mingle in the affairs of the world; and certainly not make a selection of those ideological concepts which could be helpful for the furtherance of Christian conceptions. The communists do like Christians who deal with social questions purely along their ideological lines without introducing theological categories which might lead to revisionism, i.e. a very detestable phenomenon. Equally the Orthodox Church, from its side, does not favour forms of social or political theology. In general, those in the West who object to an involvement of the church in the problems of society and are protagonists of an otherworldly religiosity have strong allies in Orthodoxy.

But the membership of the Russian Orthodox Church and other Eastern European churches in the WCC has not been without any influence upon the process of defining the issues with which the WCC should be concerned. This influence has been mainly negative: they are responsible not for what is on the agenda of the WCC, but for what is not on the agenda. Communism does not seem to represent an issue, worthwhile to discuss for Christians and Eastern Europe does not seem to raise problems in the field of church and society. The World Council does not concern itself with the socialist world, neither with its social, economic and political problems, nor with its problems in the field of human rights or with its ideology. In the programme 'Dialogue with People of Living Faiths and Ideologies' which organized a consultation on 'Churches among ideologies' in 1981, the definition of ideology has been formulated in such a way that the specific ideological aspect of the Soviet state could remain outside the discussion.

This might be explained by the fact that the Third World and Western churches have such a dominant position in this organisation that they have been able to make their concerns the only priorities. Furthermore, they have a tradition of international cooperation in the field of Life and Work which the Orthodox Churches do not have. Sometimes it is even suggested that it is useless for the WCC to deal with the problems of the communist countries because their governments are not even Christian. This is clearly a very poor argument; not only because the WCC does in fact deal with problems in countries with non-Christian governments, as is demonstrated for instance in the case of the events in India in 1975 (36), but also because it resembles the views of the Hungarian churches as mentioned above. At the basis of these views lies the assumption that the churches have no special mission in or towards socialist society.

This same point of view is expressed in the writings of the Soviet ideologists, which we have analysed and with which representatives of the churches have to conform.

The influence of the delegates from churches in Eastern Europe has not been such, even according to Marxist observers, that they have been able to dictate the agenda of the WCC, but they certainly have exerted their influence to prevent subjects, displeasing to the authorities at home, from becoming the object of study or action in the WCC or to get a prominent place on its agenda.

An astonishing confirmation of this thesis can be found in the special issue of the Ecumenical Review, dedicated to the work of 'Church and Society' (37). This symposium gives the impression that Eastern Europe does not exist. It is totally passed over and a typical phrase is: In Western Europe the church... in other cultural situations in Asia, Africa, the Americas, the Pacific Islands... (p.135). No contributions from Eastern European authors are found in this collection and it is a regrettable omission that no voice from the GDR is heard, where the Evangelical Churches -exceptional among Eastern European memberchurches- do deal with the problems of their own society and are trying to find new ways for their social witness.

The WCC does speak critically about the Western world and about Western social and political problems, but it does not speak in the same way about the socialist world: or, more precisely, does not speak about it at all.

This, however, is not a fact without importance. It is not just a regrettable omission; it can also have serious consequences for the witness of the WCC.

We have spoken of what has been called the central conviction of the WCC: its prophetic witness is an expression of the faith in the Lordship of Christ over the world and of the duty to proclaim the implications of this belief for relationships in the social and political community. The World Council should take up an independent position between the two contrasting socio-political systems which dominate the world -it should not identify itself with one of them, nor become a partisan of or a prisoner in an ideological framework. It should clearly state its understanding of the will of God and promote its application to national and international policy. This may be a too great pretension which is not realisable in the present world situation. It might even be advisable for a World Council of Churches to be more modest about its possibilities, as has been said above. But it is no good simply to forget about one part of the world and continue in the same old way for the rest of the world. That does not work in the present situation of the world, roughly divided in two antagonistic blocs, while between these blocs a vehement propaganda war is going on. One should have a realistic view of the effects of one's words and actions.

To make this clear, there now follow some examples: It is very unfortunate that the voice of the churches in the GDR is not taken more seriously in the ecumene when East-West problems are discussed. They are the only member churches in Eastern Europe which express an autonomous and realistic opinion on the way these problems should be dealt with. They constantly underline the fact that the churches have a task in their own situation, but that the ecumenical cooperation should be consultative and not directed towards common action. Bishop Werner Krusche from Magdeburg (GDR), now retired, said in an address at the sixth Assembly of the Conference of European Churches (38):

"The most difficult problem confronting the churches in the European situation is the fact that most of them live in two mutually opposed social systems. They can neither ignore this opposition nor identify themselves with it. 'Hostile' churches would be a blatant denial of Christ's reconciling work which transcends all boundaries. Yet the churches cannot be content to regard themselves as a 'third force'. In this difficult situation, they will need to keep the following points in mind in fulfilling their social diakonia:
They perform their service in and for their particular society. It is there that they do what is of service to man, by cooperating to ensure that he obtains justice. Since the situation is so different in each of the major social systems, the churches have to act independently at any given time. They will, therefore, respect one another's freedom without ever lapsing into mutal indifference. If the churches' service is to be responsible service, it must become both more constructive and, at the same time, more critical. Critical pronouncements by churches on specific social phenomena and trends in their own social and political situation are easily suspected of being, and even branded as, externally inspired: particularly when people exploit them for propaganda purposes in another social and political situation and thus treat them as ammunition in the cold war. Are there ways of preventing the misuse of such statements for propaganda purposes?"

What concerns us here are the last sentences, where he mentions the exploitation of critical pronouncements of churches for propaganda purposes in another social and political situation, thus transforming them into ammunition for use in the

Cold War. Misuse is made of critical statements of the churches when these fit into the propaganda schemes of the 'other side'. Examples are not too difficult to find and we might give one from a statement of the Hungarian churches.

The WCC has a special program on Transnational Corporations, which it regards as a Western phenomenon and which it strongly criticizes. A study-group of the Reformed Church of Hungary spoke about this project in a paper which sings the praise of the Comecon and the Eastern European communist societies and which calls on the churches to collaborate with all progressive movements (39):

> "There is a much better alternative to the multinational interests of the capitalistic world in the socialist Comecon and the peaceful transformation of economic structures... Churches must work without paying attention to sectarian or doctrinal differences with all progressive movements fighting for justice and peace."

The Western world is the object of severe moral criticism by the churches, and there are many good reasons for that. But the silence of the WCC about the socialist world is interpreted as its moral justification by the propagandists of socialism or in any case used as such. The critical dealings with the Western world and its relationship with the Third World by such an august body as the WCC is being exploited even by some member churches in their service to the socialist system. But by doing this, the critical statements are turned away from their original motivation and placed within the political framework of the competition between socialism and capitalism to serve as arguments in favour of socialism.

These statements then risk to be detached from their biblical-Christian basis and can easily 'be suspected of being externally inspired'. This tends to sharpen the reactions of the protagonists of the capitalist system, who are only too willing to see critical voices as instruments of propaganda instead of expressions of the search for a new society and of a Christian ethos.

"Are there ways of preventing the misuse of such critical statements for propaganda purposes?" exclaims Bishop Krusche, who has often had to pay the price for the misuse by part of the Western press of his independent and courageous statements. The churches' critical statements in the West about the West are also misused for propaganda purposes; but, as nobody has personally to pay a price, people do not bother much about this. Unfortunately, the price which the WCC has to pay is probably a loss of spiritual authority and influence in Western society.

It might not be possible to prevent the misuse for propaganda purposes of WCC statements, which only deal with the non-communist part of the world. But something could be done. In the first place, the WCC should denounce and rebuke the misuse of its statements for partisan political views. In the second place: 'Since the situation is so different in each of the major social systems, the churches have to act independently' (Krusche). The churches should not pretend that they can speak with one voice and function in the same way in all social systems. The WCC has its own special function as was pointed out above, but 'the churches have to perform their service in and for their particular society... without ever lapsing into mutual indifference.' A regionalisation of activities of the ecumenical movement might be the only possible way for the future.

But the WCC should also more openly rebuke and oppose all those who try to treat it as if it were an ally of their own political positions. The WCC should never allow itself to be made an exponent of any political system if it does not wish to loose its authority and the right of claiming to be an autonomous body, whose witness is rooted in the gospel and whose service for men is based on the service of Jesus Christ.

The pronouncements of some modern friends of the ecumenical movement can be very detrimental to the WCC. Just one example. In a Christmas letter to friends of a Dutch ecumenical center in Berlin, the young Dutch pastor working there wrote (Dec. 1984):

"The light is shining in the darkness and this makes us militant and opens our eyes for everything which copes with the darkness: everywhere people, movements of good will, liberation movements, peaceforces, socialist countries which try to make the best of it, anti-fascist committees, solidarity committees with the resistance in Southern Africa, with Nicaragua, women's groups, a World Council of Churches for peace and justice and somewhere on the verge our Center. Together, they form the one ecumenical movement 'The International', which will reign on earth tomorrow, that we pray, hope and expect."

It would be an interesting subject for a doctoral thesis to investigate the reflection of the WCC in the churchpress on the parish level and where the origin of the undoubtedly very varied images could be found. The one mentioned here is a highly politicized conception of the WCC, based on the idea of an apocalyptic struggle in the world between the good and the evil, between light and darkness, between progressive and reactionary forces and the parties are clearly to be identified. A concept which we have encountered also in the works of Marxists ideologists. It seems to be a clear case of the political misuse

of the WCC for propaganda purposes, but might it be possible that
this is caused by the silence of the WCC on Eastern Europe? Not
only opponents but even adherents of the WCC seem to
misunderstand the character of the witness and activities of the
WCC and explain its silence about the socialist world as a sign
of its identification with their social and political principles
and their world view.
    The churches in the European situation live in two mutually
opposed social systems, said Bishop Krusche. But this is in a way
true for most of the churches. So the WCC cannot impunitively
ignore that this fact affects its work in a very serious way. The
problems which this entails should be discussed openly and
consistently.

Involvement in social and political questions results in assimilation and system conformism

    In May 1984, the second seminar of member-churches from the
Soviet Union of the Conference of European Churches took place in
Tallinn. One of those meetings in which the Soviet churches
discuss their ecumenical policy. Sometimes not only the churches
from the USSR are called together, but also the churches from the
other socialist countries. This is a quite recent development and
little attention has up till now been given to these meetings.
The remark of an anonymous East European theologian -he must have
been from the GDR, otherwise he could not have spoken so
critically- published in a report of Faith and Order (40) is
undoubtedly referring to these meetings when it says:
    "Ecumenism in Eastern Europe is still fragile and
    inarticulate, because the ecumenical profile of the region is
    not clear, there is little opportunity to 'practise' regional
    ecumenism. Moreover, the autonomy of the regional church
    bodies cannot be safeguard against the various political
    pressures. In any case, the churches must be sure that
    ecumenism is not a trap set by the state to encourage them to
    neglect their internal, local mission for the sake of
    external, international contacts."

Not everybody in the West seems to share the opinion of this East
European ecumenist. The British General-Secretary of the
Conference of European Churches was present at the seminar in
Tallinn and addressed the meeting. He assessed highly the
significance of the seminar, at least according to the report in
the Bulletin of the Moscow Patriarchate (41), underlining that
the brotherly cooperation of the Christian Churches in the USSR
on the national level was without precedent in other European
countries and a good example for all the CEC member-churches to
follow.
It is not absolutely sure that the General-Secretary has been
quoted correctly in this bulletin, because he must be aware that

quite a few national councils of churches exist in the rest of the world. But, if so, this is a clear example of the mis-interpretation of recent, rather disturbing, ecumenical developments in Eastern Europe.

These started in Zagorsk in July 1974. Patriarch Pimen had invited leaders and representatives from the member-churches of the World Council of Churches in the communist countries of Eastern Europe to a special meeting (42). He said in his opening address in a terminology which has a remarkable similarity to that of the State's Council for Religious Affairs:

> "The Christians from the socialist countries are not only united on the common basis of a religious worldview (sic!) and unanimous struggle for a common engagement in the ecumene and the work for peace, but their common political and social convictions also bind them together as citizens of closely united socialist countries."

He called the work for peace a priority for the religious institutions (sic!)

This is said by the same Patriarch who after the Bangkok Conference on Mission and Evangelism (1973) reproached the WCC in a worthy and authentically Orthodox way (43), a trend towards one-sided and detrimental understanding of salvation in the spirit of boundless 'horizontalism' and to be ashamed to preach Christ Crucified and Resurrected. In this speech in Zagorsk he put things in a very different way, but that is not suprising for those who realize that on this occasion he was undoubtedly acting on behalf of the State Council for Religious Affairs. There is always this ambiguity in the attitude of the Russian Orthodox Church: on the one hand they accuse their Western partners of horizontalism and a one-sided leaning towards social and worldly issues; on the other hand, they constantly put peace (i.e. political) -issues at the top of the agenda. This can only be explained by the ambiguity of their position in the ecumene: the church itself looks for brotherly support and expects from its participation a strenghtening of its position, a spiritual enrichment and a help in the building-up of churchlife. But the regime has quite different expectations. It allows the church to take part in the ecumenical movement because this might be useful for its foreign policy and could embellish its image in the West and especially in Third World Countries.

The position of the Russian Orthodox Church, one of the most influential churches in the ecumenical movement, is as far as political, social, economic issues are concerned, not determined by the Christian convictions of the believers on the basis of a broad discussion and study in church-assemblies, but is determined by the Council for Religious Affairs. It seems that this was equally true for the meeting in Zagorsk. This meeting,

the first of a regular series of simular consultations, was meant to form a block of churches from the socialist countries, to exert more influence in the ecumene and to arrive at a common ecumenical policy.
This becomes quite clear from what was said about human rights. In the autumn of that same year, i.e. 1974, the WCC organized its first consultation on human rights and the Patriarch said:

> "We are convinced that Christians from socialist countries have much to say about this. As we experience the realisation of fundamental human rights and freedoms in the socialist society, we can declare: the socialistic conditions for human society fully guarantee the fundamental freedoms and rights of man; the socialist way of life creates the conditions, necessary for a full development of the human personality."

The secretary of the Hungarian Ecumenical Council also read a paper on human rights. A remarkable introduction (44) in which he said that the Christian and Marxist-Leninist conceptions of human rights coincide.

> "However, we cannot avoid to mention our own problems, because nobody will believe that we have no problems" he rightly remarked "but we have to decide what we can say about our problems and how we can say it... We could perhaps mention that in the period of revolutionary change certain rights have been violated. In the West they speak much about this as if these violations still take place . A frank statement can make it clear how energetically and consistently our governments have been in restoring and maintaining the legality. This would in any case only be advantageous for the good reputation of socialism."

A rather doubtful way to approach a brotherly consultation of Christian churches! The intention to act in the ecumenical discussion as representatives of the socialist establishment is clear. But the suggestion of unanimity of the churches in communist Europe seems to be ill-founded. The Roumanians, for instance, were not present in the first years. For these consultations of WCC member-churches in Eastern Europe have been continued. Critical voices have been heard. The secretary of the Polish Ecumenical Council, Andrzey Wojtowitcz wrote in connection with a symposion in Prague (1979) that:

> "It would be important to raise the question how the churches can bring the real problems of their country into the discussion and whether they have the necessary freedom to do so." (45)

Nor did a GDR participant favour this sort of East European meetings.

"Although the encounter with the established Marxist-Leninist socialism has given us a number of common experiences, it has certainly not marked us to such extent, that our churches have developed a specific common line of conduct."

But Moscow seems to want to bind the churches together as part of its block-policy. Helène Carrère d'Encausse has in her recent book 'Le Grand Frère - L'Union Soviétique et L'Europe Soviétisée' (Paris 1983) given a detailed description of the building-up of an integrated Soviet commonwealth in Eastern Europe, a new socialist community, according to the model of the Soviet Union, with a common attitude towards the outside world.
A chapter on the churches could easily have been added; but unfortunately, for many sovietologists the churches are a forgotten chapter. But they too are part of this enforced integration process. The Evangelical Churches in the GDR, however, were and are most unwilling to be inserted into this form of socialist ecumene and looked for support to the World Council of Churches. They let it be known that they only wanted to participate in these meetings if the Geneva secretariat would be invited to be present and to coordinate them. This was done from 1977 onwards, when the invitations were distributed via Geneva.
This was a doubtful decision, but one can understand that it would have been just as doubtful not to accede to the GDR's request. It would have made the position of the GDR churches in the East-block still more complicated. We should not too easily blame the Geneva-staff; for they too have to live under pressure from the member-churches of Eastern Europe. But why should the Vancouver-Assembly without any form of discussion approve of such a statement made in the important reference committee: (46)

"In the period 1977-1983 significant improvement has been noted in relations with member churches in Eastern Europe and other regions. The experience in Eastern Europe proved of great value in spiritual enrichment, greater awareness of churchlife and activity, and in a sense of mutual support. In the light of such achievements we are able to recognize the importance of regular, regional consultations, as well as of opportunities to share the experience of member churches living in different circumstances!"

Was there no representative who could have asked why it was necessary to make a special mention of this dubious Eastern European initiative and thus to sanction it and to make it more difficult to abstain from it for those churches which do not want to be integrated in a block of churches dominated by the Moscow State Council for Religious Affairs? With the approval of the Worldchurch this council can now continue the domestication of the churches, their submission to worldly power, their integration in a church-hostile regime, their utilisation for propagandistic aims and purposes.

One of the consequences of the involvement of East European churches in the social and political aspects of ecumenical activities has been that pressure from the side of the state-authorities has been increased. A pressure which aims at a complete assimilation. In ecumenical circles, it is often said with approval that a renewal is taking place in Orthodoxy and that the church is awakening to a new responsibility in the social field. The term used for indicating this social responsibility is 'the liturgy after the Liturgy', meant to indicate the Christian service in society. But is this liturgy after the Liturgy in the church really celebrated according to the same divine order? Or is the liturgy in society following the ritual precepts issued by other authorities? The assimilation, enforced upon the church by the regime, could probably be called a sort of 'marranisation'.
The name Marranos was given to Spanish Jews who were baptized through compulsion in the late Middle Ages, but who very often accepted Christianity only in outward appearance. Marranisation, then, is an enforced conformism to the current ritual of an ideologically uniform society. Christians may join in the life of society if they keep completely silent about their own social convictions and principles. The result is an outward conformity and an inward emigration. This process may have been stimulated by the engagement in international social activities, especially in peace-activities, where theological argumentation and political praxis are mostly rather loosely connected.

Those who have followed the development of the activities in the field of foreign relations of the Russian Orthodox Church have been able to get a clear picture of the fact that it is the Kremlin which decides the scope, the content and the intensity of these relations and which uses the church for its own diplomatic and propagandistic ends. The regional consultations of East European churches were undoubtedly convened to unify the ecumenical policy of these churches. The Patriarch denied at the Zagorsk meeting in rather vehement terms, that it would be the intention to form a block of churches in the ecumenical movement. But other authoritative pronouncements clearly show that the ecumenical policy of the Moscow Patriarchate is based on the presumption that blocks exist and that the churches act as part of a block. The Patriarch himself remarked in an address to a Finnish audience, in 1974 (47) that:

"It would be useful for the World Council of Churches to take note of the views of a large body of churches and numerous Christians, who have combined their efforts towards the building of peace within the framework of the Christian Peace Conference."

A diplomatic way of mentioning the existence in the WCC of a specific pressure-group. Metropolitan Yuvenaly presented a report at a Consultation of Orthodox Churches with representatives of the World Council of Churches, Sofia, May 1981 on 'Prospects of Orthodox Contribution to the WCC Activities' (48). He proposed a revision of the voting system, used in the WCC to decide questions of a doctrinal character. An acceptable proposal, but what draws our attention here is one of his arguments. He said:

"In considering and deciding questions of a political and social significance, the practical experience of the World Council of Churches has produced an unwritten rule and practice of observing the principle of equality in composing appropriate groups of equal numbers of representatives of the churches of the West, of the East and of the developing countries. Experience also proves that the World Council decisions in the political and social fields can only be effective if they are worked out and adopted on the principles of parity by all these three sides participating in the WCC activities."

According to Yuvenaly, there are three blocks or sides and each block is supposed to present a common opinion on social and political matters. We may notice the similarity of his conception and that of the Soviet ideologists (see above). The consultations of East European member-churches thus serve the unification of the views and positions of these churches and their harmonisation with those of the State Council for Religious Affairs. They contribute in this way not only to the formation of a block in the World Council of Churches according to political lines; but also to a strengthening of the process of integration of the churches in the system. It is very interesting to notice that the request for a broader participation of the Orthodox Churches in the ecumenical movement coïncides with the request for a broader participation of the churches from socialist countries. On the one hand as Orthodox Churches, on the other hand as churches from socialist countries, the Russians demand a larger share of responsibility in the World Council of Churches. More attention should be given, according to a June 1982 Budapest Consultation of Churches in socialist countries (49), to the contribution which these churches can give to the life and activities of the Council.

"Experience of the churches in socialist countries can be of some use and benefit to Christians in the Third World where society is in the process of rapid social and ideological change in the direction of socialist order. Closely related to the problem of social justice and human dignity, the

Christian response to the model of socialist society will be of paramount interest for brothers and sisters in Western Europe, North America and in developing countries... the churches in socialist countries have a lot to say and do in the area of peace, where they have wide experience and fine achievements."

It seems that, here, the intention has been formulated to make a better use of the World Council of Churches as a means to improve the image of socialism in the world and to have a greater influence on the peace-initiatives of the Council. Not much is made known of the content of the deliberations in these meetings; but, what is known confirms the impression that Eastern European church representatives wish to have more influence in the ecumenical programmes and activities in order to be able to better serve the cause which they are bound to serve. Pressure is exerted on them to achieve homogeneity of action in the ecumenical movement: a step which is fully in line with Soviet policy which seeks cohesion in Eastern European activities in the international sphere. It seems extremely difficult for churches in Eastern Europe not to conform to this pressure, as the Evangelical Churches in the GDR are experiencing. Their freedom of action in regard to social and political problems has been even more limited by these consultations of East European churches. They are pressured into conformity with the Moscow-line and forced to act as the mouth-piece of party politics.
The statement of the Vancouver Assembly, quoted above, which seems to sanctify this process, must be seriously deplored.

The integrity of the representatives

A problem which any ecumenist who writes about the situation of the churches in Eastern Europe has to face is this: how to write about the political captivity of churches in Eastern Europe without challenging the integrity of the representatives of these churches.
    In this cruel sea one can founder on either of two rocks. One is the simplistic suspicion that every representative from the church in a communist country is a secret agent of the police. A CCIA officer, mentioned on p.115 seems to assume that even in ecumenical circles this opinion can be found. He writes that especially:

"the leaders of the Russian Orthodox Church have been portrayed as agents of the Soviet Government, through whose activities the WCC itself becomes a tool of Soviet policies."

In general this is not correct and ecumenically engaged Christians have always opposed this allegation: although they are conscious of the fact that in church delegations there will usually be a government official to supervise the conduct of the delegates. Just as every church body in the Soviet Union from the national to the local level is supervised by the State Secretariat for Religious Affairs and nothing can happen without its consent, so does evidently a church delegation not escape the watchful eye of this state-council, whose task it is 'to work with the religious organisations in establishing international relations." The well-known Furov-report, issued by this state-council (50), speaks about the differing degrees of loyalty of the bishops towards the government and towards the church. And this can be confirmed by those who are personally engaged in ecumenical contacts with the Russian churches. Simplistic generalisations are not only inflicting injustice upon a number of faithful and loyal churchmen, but give rise to equally simplistic reactions of those who assume that there is nothing extraordinary and sinister in the state-church relations of the Soviet Union.

The other rock on which one can founder is to project one's own personal freedom, natural in a Western-shaped democratic society, onto representatives from the Soviet-Union. This attitude seems to be typical, for example, of some press-representatives.

An interesting commentary was written by Nicolas Lossky, Professor at the Institute Saint-Serge and a member of an Orthodox parish of the Moscow Patriarchate in France, after the visit of a Russian church delegation to France at the invitation of the French Roman Catholic bishops in November 1979 (51). A visit like this could be regarded as an exemplary paradigm: a dialogue purely on church matters and an exchange of experiences between the churches about theological education.
Nevertheless, the visit has given rise to some controversy because of press-interviews in which members of the delegation were asked about the recent arrest of Christians in their country. The answers were either evasive or in strict conformity to the official statements by the government.

"But," writes Lossky, to demand from Russian bishops to condemn an aspect of the policy of their country, is that not a case of choosing the wrong partner? A very subtle means of compromising the church is to make its responsible spokesmen speak about difficult subjects (e.g. the non-respecting of human rights) before the Western press... If we Westerners make bishops speak about subjects on which they have 'a lesson to recite' we expose them to shame in the eyes of the world, which is exactly what the persecuting Soviet power wants. And we, who denounce the infringements of the human rights, make them involuntarily the accomplices of those who persecute."

Those who do not take account of the specific position of Russian churchmen at home and abroad often achieve the opposite of what they intend. The same sort of discussion was started by Paul Mojzes in an American publication edited by an ecumenical association related to the National Council of Churches in the USA, which can hardly be suspected of being hostile to the ecumenical movement (52). He was disturbed by the fact that a Russian church delegation invited to the USA by a group called Bridges to Peace in October 1984 'did not tell the truth about conditions, particularly the religious conditions, in their country. Why? What makes them say things which are blatantly false?" He then enumerates a number of possible explanations. They are cautious because anything which is published can get them, their loved ones, and their churches into trouble; their concept of religious liberty is different; they may have fallen prey to the same propaganda manipulation to which the citizens of their country have been so massively subjected:

> "One may add to this interpretation that those clergy who are chosen to travel on such missions are beholden to the state authorities. Such travel is a rare privilege. They are carefully screened and briefed... They also know that the disadvantages to themselves, and more importantly to their churches, if they step out of line, are simply not worth taking such risks (...) The reason for this behaviour is terror."

Mojzes believes that this terror still exists in the Soviet Union; but now it is selective.

> "Knowledge that this terror can be unleashed at any moment against any given person is a sufficient threat against all but the most brave. Among Soviet believers there are such people of courage. But the vast majority, including the leaders, chose a path of prudent compliance with the requests of those with the power to unleash the terror."

He also remarks that both Western conservatives and liberals tend to be blind in one eye: thus failing to notice one part of Soviet reality. Conservatives fail to see the changes. Liberals fail to see the continuities.

> "The change is that terror is no longer general. That is an improvement. The continuity is that terror, now selective, is nevertheless still terror. Couple this terror with the overwhelming amount of governement propaganda (few or no alternative viewpoints available) and one gets a fairly adequate theoretical interpretation for the behaviour of many of the visiting clergy."

It is good that these voices are to be heard in the ecumenical movement, especially when they come from those who are personally engaged in the ecumenical relationships with Eastern Europe.

We should strongly oppose those who, on the basis of these realistic judgements, plead for a rupture of contacts with church people from the Soviet Union. We should invite, receive and visit them, but, if we wish to help them, we should not have naive ideas about their predicament. In a small discussion-group at an international meeting, one of the courageous Russian church representatives exclaimed: for you it is easy to talk, you do not feel the hot breath of the atheists in your neck!

The Russian Orthodox Church is not a fallen but a captive church, and we should take this into account while converging with its representatives.

In an essay entitled 'Between Loyalty and Martyrdom' (53) published ten years ago, the author did attack strongly the concept of the 'underground church', portrayed as the true church over against the 'false leaders' of the offically-legalized churches. Thus we cannot qualify the leadership of the church even if we realize its extremely complicated position. In all matters circa sacra, that is to say which do not directly concern the content of the faith and the liturgy, the church is subjected to the whims of a hostile regime and has no independence. Its loyalty to the powers that be is constantly supervised and has to be made explicit at every occasion. Metropolitan Sergy, later elected as Patriarch, issued a declaration of loyalty to the Soviets in 1927 in which he explained:

"We want to be Orthodox and at the same time we want to accept the Soviet Union as our earthly fatherland and to be citizens of the Union 'not only for wrath, but also for conscience's sake' (Romans 13:5)... only world-estranged dreamers can imagine that so great a fellowship as the Orthodox Church can hide itself from the State and so exist in the State."

Although much criticized in those days, this statement has opened the only possible way for the church in the Soviet Union, a very difficult and stony path indeed.

Such is, however, the situation: and we must try to exercise restraint in our judgement. Critical voices from the church community itself penetrate to us, especially since the sixties. This inner opposition is important for it can protect the official church from going too far in harmony with the authorities. It does even lead the authorities sometimes into small concessions; because they do not want the coming into existence of groups outside the church on which they have no grip. There are bishops and priests who reach the point where they can no longer accept to constantly compromise and be humiliated. But this is at the same time the point where loyalty turns into martyrdom and the terror strikes. Who are we to challenge the brothers to become martyrs?

The Russian priest S. Zheludkov once wrote:
"The official Church cannot be an isle of freedom in a completely uniformly organized society which is controlled from one single centre. The Russian Church is confronted by the dilemma: either to go underground, which in the existing system is unthinkable, or to conform in one way or other to the system and to make use in the meantime of such possibilities as are still left open to the Church. The Russian hierarchy has chosen the second possibility, because there was no other choice."

But, since the entrance of the church representatives from the Soviet Union in the WCC, our problems have become increasingly complicated. It is no longer sufficient to come to a well-balanced objective and nuanced view of the plight of a far-away church. We are faced with the question of how to cooperate with it. Some facts have then to be taken into account.

1. The specific ideas of the regime in regard to the task of the church and its freedom. The former (till 1984) chairman of the State-Secretariat for Religious Affairs Kuroyedov paraphrased the freedom of the church in these words: The church with us is free and independent in the fulfillment of its only function -to satisfy the religious needs of the believers.
2. The regime has discovered that the church might be a useful instrument in furthering the aims of Soviet foreign policy abroad. We can read in Nauka i Religya (54)
"The churchworkers from the Soviet Union and the fraternal countries inform the religious public opinion in the West about the politics of the socialist countries, the status of the general ideas of their countries, especially of those of the believers, in questions of war and peace."
That there could be a difference of opinion between believers and others in the Soviet Union has, however, never been acknowledged by the authorities. The opinion of the believers is supposed to be identical with those of the ruling party.
3. Church representatives abroad do not dispose of more freedom than other citizens, either at home or abroad. Their contacts are subject to the guidance and supervision of the state. Those who doubt this will have to prove their point against all experts on Soviet law and Soviet life.

But even those who accept these facts can and should use all the possibilities of contacts with the churches from the Soviet Union which present themselves. The churches should not let themselves be hindered by any wall of division. But they have to realize that with 'hostages' (N. Lossky) of a hostile regime they cannot freely discourse on all subjects. In all matters of faith and order we have a lot to discuss and the churches can express independent positions in this field. It can equally be useful to come to an exchange of opinions and ideas on social and political questions. For Russians it is a good thing to have a window open to the rest of the world, however small this may be; it might help them to change their conceptions which are very one-sided and influenced by propaganda; and it might even make them more critical about their situation. For Westerners, it is equally useful to meet Soviet people, to get acquainted with their ways of life and thinking and, which is often the case, to begin to like them. We should not be too anxious if our contacts have a certain propagandistic value for the regime and if churchmen travelling abroad can cause some misunderstandings about their real situation. People in the West are generally critical enough not to allow themselves to be misled, and it is not forbidden here to correct false or misleading information. It will also be useful to discuss whether we can come to common convictions as Christians, living in different social systems about questions of life and work of the churches and general problems of humanity with which we are all concerned.

The study on faith, science and technology presents a good example of such a general problem, which concerns us all and may not be too directly linked with the usual themes of propaganda. It then becomes, unfortunately, clear how restricted the possibilities of the Russian churches in fact are. They have in their present circumstances no discussions in their own church between believers and scientists; and such studies represent for them a good way of getting acquainted with problems which concern Christian life and ethics directly, but on which they have not much to contribute because of their lack of experience in these matters.

But, as was explained above, the cooperation of churches in the WCC embraces more than just the study of confessional questions and ethical problems. And the member churches have not been willing to restrict their common activities in the WCC, in view of the special position and limited possibilities of the Russian Orthodox Church, to those only. On the contrary, social and political questions have been given a more prominent place and the urge to take action or make pronouncements on issues of direct political relevance has increased. Then, however, the captivity or the lack of autonomy and independence or the fact that the representatives are screened and briefed or that they have a hidden agenda or have their lesson to recite, or in whatever other way one may describe their position, begins to play a role. Then one has to pose the question of the aims and intentions of the regime in allowing the churches to participate in ecumenical activities, while they officially recognize only one function for the church; namely: the satisfaction of the religious needs of believing comrades. What are these representatives commissioned to do and what impact do they have on the ecumene?

People may come to different conclusions; but the question itself seems to be fully justified and honest and need not be inspired by a feeling of mistrust of the integrity of church representatives, but finds its origin in an insight into their plight. It is even curious that this is not more openly and consistently discussed in ecumenical circles.

It is true that the churches from the Soviet Union can only maintain ecumenical contacts within the framework and the limits which are laid down by the government, and that they cannot publicly speak about the pressure under which they are living and have to operate. But are their partners conscious of what they are doing when involving the representatives of these churches in all their activities? Are they not unintentionally contributing in this way to the marranisation of the church and its fuller assimilation in the policy of the regime?

In the coming years the collaboration with the churches from the Soviet Union and the communist countries will reach a critical point when more staff-members will be put forward by them to be nominated. The pressure to do this clearly exists; but what will happen when, for instance, one third of the staff actually consists of people from the socialist part of the world, in accordance with the three 'sides' or blocks of which the WCC is supposed to consist? It is clear that the Evangelical Churches of the GDR would be able to provide the ecumenical organisation with politically independent staff-members. But the other Eastern European countries do not take the initiative to recommend them. Their state-secretariats would not favour it; and the exceptional position of the GDR churches in the communist world has not made them exceedingly popular in leading church circles in Eastern Europe either.

There are, of course, instances in the life of the WCC-secretariat of fruitful collaboration with people from Eastern European countries. Some of them have even given the impression that they could rise above the limitations on free expression and independent behaviour to which all their co-citizens are subjected. But the experience of Unesco should not be forgotten. A former British Assistant Director General, Richard Hoggart (55) writes:

"The Soviets do find it almost impossible to believe that a member of the Secretariat is not also a member of his national civil service, or at least a dutiful mouthpiece and reporter."

It certainly goes also for church representatives, that those recommended and commissioned for jobs in the WCC must be acceptable to the State Secretariat and that, in questions which are not purely confessional, they cannot be regarded as politically independent people. For the best of them, if ever they get as far as being chosen for such a sensitive post in the international sphere, it will not be an enviable position. All those who have responsible positions in the Russian Orthodox Church are experiencing the dilemma of conflicting loyalties and of compromising between the exigencies of the church which they serve and the church-hostile state to which they are subjected. This will, to a still greater extent, apply to a church servant in an international body. Is it reasonable to bring someone into this situation? Or should we envisage a reconstruction of the international ecumenical body, in which we collaborate with the Russians and other East-Europeans, in such a way that only those questions appear on the agenda where the churches can speak with their own voice and that their political authorities lose their direct interests?

There are reasons to doubt the willingness of the churches to consider this, although the WCC is admonished from different sides to change its policy. So, for instance, by Nikolas Lossky, member of Faith and Order and expert on orthodox theology and Russian church life (56). But, in general, there is, notwithstanding the many mostly rather superficial contacts a tremendous lack of real insight into the situation of the Russian and other churches: and little information is made available by ecumenical bodies (while what information there is, is often treated as suspect). Much will have to be done before the Christian precept of 'suffering with those who suffer' will lead to a readiness to change the pattern of ecumenical cooperation in the WCC in such a way that it can really serve the life and witness of the churches in captivity.

NOTES

1. J.A. Hebly, The Russians and the World Council of Churches. Belfast, 1978.
2. Die Europäische Christenheit in der heutigen Welt. Nyborg 1959. Zürich, 1960.
3. J.A. Hebly, o.c., p.25, 89, 118, 155; p 87-89 minutes of the meating in Utrecht.
4. Ecumenical Review, Vol.XXI no.2, 1969, p.119.
5. Section II; also quoted by Leon Hoewell, Acting in Faith. The World Council of Churches since 1975. WCC, Geneva, 1982, p.42
6. "Contemporary Ecumenism", edited by the Academy of Sciences of the USSR, 1972
7. Nastolnaja Kniga Ateista, Moskva 1975, 4, p.414
8. Khristianskij Ekumenizm, Moskva 1980, p. 29. 157
9. Nauka i Religiya, 7 (1975), p.84
10. Nauchnyj ateizm, Moskva 1978, 4, p.99
11. Stimme der Orthodoxie, 1972, 12, p. 53f
12. Ecumenical Review XXI no.2, 1969, p.127
13. See: Religion in Communist Dominated Areas, Vol. XIII, 1974, p.140-145
14. London 1956, p.106
15. The World Council of Churches and the Struggle between East and West, Vol. IX no. 13, 25 July 1949
16. The first Assembly of the World Council of Churches, New York, 1949, p.91-95
    O.F. Nolde: The Churches and the Nations, 1970, p.176
17. Ungarische Kirchliche Pressedienst (UKP) Vol. XIX, 1967
18. Ungarische Kirchliche Nachrichen (UKN) Vol. XX, 1968, p.79-80
19. Contribution to Nyborg VI, UKN, Vol. XXIII, 1971, p.13
20. UKN, Vol. XXIII, 1971. p.17
21. Quoted by the Journal of the Moscow Patriarchate, 1984-5. p. 67
22. The Journal of the Moscow Patriarchate 1982-1, p.69-74. 1982-2, p. 67-72
23. See note 11
24. See note 11
25. CCPD Documents 18, Nov. 1980, IV, p.7
26. See note 11
27. Stimme der Orthodoxie 10, 1976, p.41
28. Evangelische Informationen, 16-8-1984
29. Patriarch Pimen of Moscow. An orthodox view on contemporary ecumenism. In: E.G. Patelos, o.c., p.334, 336
30. 1983-10, p.538
31. Oldham's method in Abrecht's Hands. Ecumenical Review, Vol. XXXVII no. 1, Jan. 1985
32. A.E. Levitin-Krasnov, Die Glut deiner Hände. Memoiren eines russischen Christen. Luzern, 1980, p. 271

33. Jacques Ellul, Trahison de l'Occident, 1975, p. 29
34. See: L.E. Odell, The Church and Society explosion in Latin America; J.C. Benett, The Geneva Conference of 1966 as a Climatic Event. Ecumenical Review Vol. XXXVII no. 1, Jan. 1985, p.26-33, 34-39
35. CCPD Documents IV, 18 Nov. 1980, pp. 22,7
36. See: Ron O'Grady, Bread and Freedom. Understanding and acting on human rights. Geneva 1979, p. 41
37. Ecumenical Review Vol. XXXVII, no. 1, Jan 1985
38. Servants of God, Servants of Men. This happened at Nyborg VI, Geneva 1971, p. 176
39. CCPD Documents IV, 18 Nov. 1980, p. 6-11
40. Church and State. Faith and Order Paper 85, 1978, p.111
41. Information Bulletin-Moscow Patriarchate, External Church Relations Department no. 6, 25 Mai 1984
42. Stimme der Orthodoxie 10, 1974, p.2-7
43. C.G. Patalos ed., The Orthodox Church in the Ecumenical Movement. Documents and Statements 1902-1975, Geneva 1978, p.47-52
44. See: Preparatory material for the St. Pölten Consultation on Human Rights, Oct. 1974
45. See: J.A. Hebly, Strijd om Vrede, Den Haag, 1983, p.40
46. David Gill ed., Gathered for Life. Official Report VI Assembly WCC. Geneva 1983, p.116
47. See note 29
48. The Journal of the Moscow Patriarchate, 1981-10, p.61
49. Ecumenical Press Service, July 1982, 49/23
50. Rapport secret au Comité sur l'Etat de l'Eglise en USSR, Paris 1980.
51. N. Lossky, Plaidoyer pour l'Eglise orthodoxe russe. Istina 1981, p.122. Autour d'un voyage. Unité des Chrétiens, nr. 41, Janvier 1981
52. Occasional Papers on Religion in Eastern Europe, edited by Christians Associated For Relationships with Eastern Europe, Vol. IV no.6, Dec, 1984
53. In: J.A. Hebly, Protestants in Russia, Belfast 1976; See also: J.A. Hebly, The Russians and the WCC, p.140
54. 1984, 7, p.54
55. An idea and its servants. Unesco from within. London 1978, p.45
56. Nicolas Lossky: Keston College, Pays de l'Est, Conseil Oecuménique des Eglises - Service Orthodoxe de Presse (SOP) no.96, Mars 1985, p. 10-14

Chapter V

THE WORLD COUNCIL OF CHURCHES AND RELIGIOUS LIBERTY

The identity of the World Council of Churches is not easy to define. The Constitution speaks about the confession of its constituency: churches which confess the Lord Jesus Christ as God and Saviour according to the Scriptures ...- and about its functions and purposes: to call the churches to the goal of visible unity in one faith, to facilitate their common witness and to express their common concern in the service of human need.

But these formal principles do not imply that there exists unanimity among the memberchurches how they can and should use this common instrument, which they have created to serve their ecumenical purposes. For some of them it should mainly serve the search for a new relationship among the churches in view of their ultimate unity, others see it as a form of practical collaboration of believers in the struggle for peace, as the spearhead of a movement for social, cultural and economic change in world society, as a meeting-place of churchleaders or of partners in service and so on.

Looking at the activities of the WCC one sees a great variety of studyprogrammes and working-projects which often follow one other in rapid succession and one gets the impression of a lively organism, readily taking up new initiatives and responding to new challenges. This complexity does not make it easier to define exactly 'What in the world is the World Council of Churches'. (1) It has many aspects, it issues a variety of statements and reports, it has many different representatives and shows the world and its own memberchurches many faces. It will be clear that not all its activities are equally appreciated by all its adherents, but that this world-wide fellowship of so diverse churches exists in our world, torn apart by cultural, racial and political tensions and by national, religious and ideological passions, is in itself a most remarkable and happy phenomenon. The best description, probably, is to call it the center of a network of interchurch-relations and of the many concerns of its memberchurches. Even the most active participants are not always capable of surveying its many-sided activities or to share in all the concerns which are brought into the discussion. Russian Orthodox representatives often seem to be as puzzled as some traditional Western churchmen by, for instance, the issue of feminism which at present is taking up a rather prominent place.

The question of the identity becomes more complicated still when we ask what the diachrone identity of the WCC is. The extension of the number of memberchurches and the shifting of powercentres have changed the character of the organization. "The new members brought with them perceptions which were at variance with those of the WCC's 'old guard'. An immense learning process took place which gradually brought a change in the positions taken by the Council." (2) writes one of the staff-members. The Council has changed considerably since its creation in 1948 and its perceptions and positions differ, according to this staff-member, from those in the early years. To understand this we have to take note of what is said in the Constitution about public statements:

> "In the performance of its functions, the Council through its Assembly or through its Central Committee may publish statements upon any situation or issue with which the Council or its constituent churches may be confronted. While such statements may have great significance and influence as the expression of the judgment or concern of so widely representative a Christian body, yet their authority will consist only in the weight which they carry by their own truth and wisdom..."

Statements of the WCC have no formal authority, but can only function in so far as they are received and accepted by the churches on the basis of the truth and wisdom they contain according to the readers. But there are no formal rules for this process of reception and it seems that one just has to find out whether a declaration, which one might deem to testify of much truth and wisdom, is still accepted in the ecumenical fellowship or whether it has been filed in the historical archives. Does this mean that there is no diachrone identity, that there is no continuity in the young ecumenical tradition? Could it be that what once was called 'the heart or the central conviction of the ecumenical movement' later on lost all relevance? Some declarations of earlier days like the Toronto-declaration (1950) about the ecclesiological status of the WCC seem still to be widely accepted, but what about the Declarations on Religious Liberty, issued by the Assemblies of Amsterdam (1948) and New Delhi (1961)?

What is the diachrone identity of the WCC on the issue of religious liberty and what is at present the authority of these statements? Can they still function as guidelines for the work in this field? No other declarations have been published since by 'so widely representative a Christian body'. The 'Declaratio de libertate religiosa. Dignitatis Humanae' of the Second Vatican Council has shown that a real convergence has come about among the Christian churches regarding their views on social religious liberty (3). It is moreover a fact that there have never been any requests from the side of churches in Eastern Europe to revise these declarations, although they raise an obligatory protest when the declarations are applied to their situation.

The question is of more than passing importance, because in speaking of the situation of the churches in Eastern Europe it is very useful to have a sound basis in Christian principles on religious liberty. It must constantly be made clear by those who speak, publish and inform about the life of these churches and try to evaluate their position in society, that they are not inspired by political motives -the accusation of anti-communist agitation and cold-war propaganda is repeatedly raised against them in the Soviet media- but find their standards and guidelines in the great declarations of world Christianity, which express a commonly held position on social religious liberty.

It may be that a too emphatic public judgment on the implementation of the rights of religious liberty in communist countries, is not deemed possible for an international church organisation in which churches from these countries participate. W.A. Visser 't Hooft, one of the 'old guard', wrote as early as 1949 that 'our inevitable and necessary reactions to the infringements of religious liberty and to totalitarian practices will create formidable tensions'.(4) It seems that the WCC wishes at all costs to avoid this sort of tensions, which came to the surface for a short while at the Nairobi Assembly, but it has constantly admonished the churches in the West to pursue the study of the situation as regards religious liberty in Eastern Europe. Another 'old-timer' E.C. Blake, wrote as General-Secretary in 1972 an open letter to the Reformed Churches in the Netherlands concerning human rights in Eastern Europe. In this letter he stressed the need for better information:

"The many restrictions on churches in Eastern Europe make it difficult to ask these churches to publish more about their life themselves, but studies made and reported in the West can help to lay a solid base for real knowledge, understanding and effective help."

This letter has been a sort of 'letter of instruction' for some students of Eastern Europe to take this work in hand, with the intention of stimulating the knowledge, understanding and help of these churches. They felt this to be part of their ecumenical mission. But does the WCC still accept its own declarations on religious liberty as valid statements which can function as sound basic principles for students and institutes which deal with Eastern Europe? May we still suppose that there exists a diachrone identity in this aspect of the activities of the WCC or has a complete shift of policy come about?

Two rather disquieting developments may be observed:

a. In the first place the main declarations have been strongly criticized in more recent studypapers (5). According to these publications, they reflect cold-war tensions and Western liberal-individualistic conceptions, and are as such apparantly of very limited importance. Historically the prevailing concept of human rights is regarded as a product of the French and American revolutions and nothing is said of the long tradition of suffering and oppression of Christians belonging to minority groups in Europe. The history of the struggle for religious liberty in Europe has been long and painful (the Huguenots; the Moravian Brethren; the British dissenters; The Russian Baptists and many others) and just as the Declaratio of the Vatican Council, the Amsterdam and New Delhi declarations may in European perspective be seen as the expressions of a final discovery of long neglected Christian truth and ethos.

They are, however, now depicted as weapons, designed for the cold war and as sublimated expressions of Christian egoism, which wants to restore forlorn privileges and regain former positions of power. But in that case one is providing justification for the ancient accusation that any effort for the implementation of religious liberty rights is political agitation and a threat to peaceful co-existence. When religious liberty is not seen as a basic human right, it can be devalued into a product of the bourgeois-revolution and linked to the rights of the private ownership of the means of production and free trade. Religious liberty has then become a completely Western concept and its advocates can be unmasked as the lackeys of capitalistic exploitation and neo-colonial domination. Instead of being the motor of human liberation and emancipation religious liberty risks being considered a tool of human oppression. When the WCC declarations on religious liberty are considered mainly as a product of Western culture and the furthering of its implementation as a tool of Western politics, then we are moving into a sphere which seems to be alien to that in which they were originally conceived. It is self-evident that the study and discussion of the Christian conception of religious liberty has to be pursued and that the experiences and biblical insights of other peoples have to be taken into account. The Christian basis and the clear biblical anthropological background have certainly to be more fully unfolded. The endeavour of the Central Committee (1979) to start a renewed study of this issue has failed completely but should be pursued by theologians.

For the time being it might be a wise policy to respect the work done by the 'old guard' and to resist even subtle forms of its defamation.

b. Another development which is very disquieting is the denial of support which those who are committed to the cause of religious liberty in Eastern Europe, encounter in the World Council of

Churches. The report by a staff-member of the Commission of the Churches on International Affairs (CCIA) already mentioned, contains some very biased remarks and seems to put seriously into doubt the honest intentions of a number of past and present ecumenists. Two passages must be mentioned. In speaking about the post-war developments in Europe the author states, that

"many Christians in the West saw the possibility of propitiating for their sins of omission during fascist rule by turning to a fervent commitment to the religious liberty of their sister churches in Eastern Europe. And in doing so they played directly into the hands of a political manoeuvre which has succeeded in tearing the continent even further and irreparably asunder, a confrontation which has since been called 'Cold War'."

From a historical point of view this is a completely false statement, as the author of this essay tried to show elsewhere (6), and it not only disavows the 'old guard' of European ecumenists, but is even insulting for all those who suffered under and fought against fascist rule. The involvement of the generation, engaged in the ecumene in the days of the First Assembly and thereafter in the struggle for liberty and democratic values against fascism, had sharpened their awareness of the fate of those who are victims of injustice and enslavement in totalitarian regimes. The ecumenical generation, which cared for the fate of the sisterchurches in Eastern Europe can be made responsible for tearing asunder our continent only by those who have a completely distorted view of European ecumenical history.

A second deplorable passage in the CCIA booklet speaks about the contribution of the Russian Orthodox Church to the programme of the WCC and of what its leaders expected from their Western counterparts: understanding of their political environment and of their theological contributions.

"These expectations have to some extent been satisfied, but repeatedly also disappointed. After more than twenty years, there can still be found a considerable level of mistrust, which has been fed by forces hostile to the ecumenical movement. Especially the Russian Orthodox Church has been the object of such hostility, its leaders having been portrayed as agents of the Soviet government, through whose activities the WCC itself becomes a tool of Soviet policies. This has been the stock argument of the South African government, for example, which attempts by this means to discredit the WCC."

These sentences are taken from a chapter which discusses the Nairobi Assembly (1975) and the public debate on religious liberty in the Soviet Union which took place during that

Assembly. It is necessary to keep that in mind, because when reading it out of context one might suppose that the subject of discussion is the attitude of some crusade organisations which are not only fervently anti-communist but also anti-ecumenical. But we are moving within the ecumenical fellowship and we take note of the suggestion (or insinuation) that when one speaks about religious liberty in communist countries this can be interpreted as a sign of hostility towards the ecumenical movement and the Russian Orthodox Church. We have spoken about the accusation of church leaders being agents of the Soviet government elsewhere in this collection, but it is essential to rectify the misunderstanding that raising the suject of religious liberty can be interpreted as an hostile attack on the churches concerned. Usually they are regarded as the victims and not the authors of the restrictions on social religious liberty and the Nairobi debate has been regarded by many as a sign of solidarity with Christian believers in the Soviet Union; which indeed it was meant. But whatever this whole passage with its different allegations might mean, it raises the suspicion that those who apply the declarations of the WCC on religious liberty to the situation in Eastern European countries are out of order in the ecumenical fellowship and are at the best unintentionally out of naivety, but otherwise wilfully, part of a dark anti-ecumenical conspiracy. It would be unwise to attach too much importance to this pamplet, but it is indicative of a climate which is not very susceptible to an open discussion of the issue of religious liberty in Eastern Europe and of the problems which the ecumenical collaboration with the churches in that region involves.

The question of the diachrone identity of the WCC in the field of study and action on social religious liberty is thus not so easy to answer. The least one can say is, that the profile of the WCC in this field is very low - certainly as far as Eastern Europe is concerned. The main declarations were republished in 1980 (7) but one gets the impression that this was more an act of piety for the past or a reminder of former engagements, than a reflection of the importance which is attached to them at the present moment. The 'old guard' has certainly reason to wonder whether all changes have been for the good.

Critics of the World Council of Churches

We have to dwell a short while on the curious fact that in the WCC the theory is going round of the existence of a conspiracy of WCC opponents, highly organised and inspired by political forces hostile to the ecumenical movement. We have already quoted the remark of a WCC officer, author of the pamphlet on human rights, which distinguished itself by style and content from the usually well-balanced and very readable Genevan publications. But there are other instances, for example in the report Nairobi to Vancouver (8) where in a chapter on the much discussed Programme to Combat Racism it is said: 'There are clear indications pointing to well-planned and well-organised attempts to discredit the work -in fact the very existence- of the WCC, through a distortion of the aims and nature of this programme.'

The main passage however, which drew our attention and on which we have pondered a long time is to be found in the report of the Policy Reference Committee to the Vancouver Assembly (9):

> "Critics from outside the Council fall into two categories: general misinformed comment and leafletting on ecumenical events, and highly organised, often politically motivated hostile campaigns of criticism of the Council and its work. Internal criticism also takes two forms: that which is concerned for constructive discussion of genuine theological differences, and negative challenges to the very purpose and programmes of the Council. This latter criticism is most destructive of the life of the Council and could call into question the essential meaning of membership in the WCC...
> Such criticisms, however, are inevitable. While not in themselves a guarantee that the Council is faithfully following the way of the cross, it has to be stated that the link between costliness and discipleship is unmistakably clear, and in the end the work of the Council will be judged by other standards than those of its critics."

A very remarkable statement indeed! Everybody who has spent the main part of his life in ecumenical work knows about critics of the WCC and had to devote a lot of his time explaining about the ecumene, its history, goals, programmes, activities and its relevance for the local and national churches. Many might agree with the exclamation of Sir Kenneth Grubb, director of the CCIA up till 1968, in his autobiography (10): "I do not grudge the time which I have given to the ecumenical movement. What is the point of doing that when it is too late? I think I would have been happier in the interior of South America." His friends called him very critical of the WCC, but he writes: "It may be, but the Council need not be sensitive or thin-skinned." Reading the passage from the Vancouver report one gets the impression that this sound advice has been neglected. Why this defensive and irritated reaction? The ecumenical leadership must 'know that a strategy of just blaming the critics is neither going to work nor worthy of a Christian movement." (11) And although the Moderator of the Central Committee noticed in his report at Vancouver (12) that there is 'growing documentation indicating that persons and groups who do not want certain kinds of issues raised or discussed are deliberately seeking to misinterpret or misrepresent the Council.' he also warned to 'avoid becoming

overly defensive' and said that the Council is willing to be
challenged by the member churches.

But what are we to make of the Vancoucer statement? How to
distinguish a critic from within from a critic from without? Some
of the former adherents of the WCC have turned into rather severe
critics, maybe because they were not able to follow the changing
pattern of ecumenical life and interests. But why this suggestion
of 'highly organised, often politically motivated hostile
campaigns of criticism?' Is there anywhere behind this idea of a
political maffia aimed at undermining the WCC, the same sort of
concept as was expressed by our young Dutch pastor, mentioned
above on page 88. He saw the world divided into two opposing
camps of good guys and bad guys. The forces for the good included
among others: the World Council of Churches, the liberation
movements and the socialist countries. It is rather curious that
those who do show a mistrust of the way in which some delegates
from communist countries present their political environment,
those who have differing opinions about liberation movements and
those who criticise the work of the WCC, are thrown into one and
the same basket. It is difficult to assume that in general the
representatives of the memberchurches in Vancouver cherish this
concept of a world divided into clearly definable progressive and
reactionary forces, so dear to the marxist ideologists. But some
people who are in a position to influence the drafting of
statements might be injected by it. It is, however, quite
natural, given the varigated scala of activities of the WCC and
the choice of its priorities, that critical voices will always be
heard. And when the churches express themselves on political
issues and take up definite positions in highly controversial
political questions, they might know that those who have
differing views on those matters will oppose and contradict them.
The political arena is not more peaceful than the confessional
one. There is no reason to turn this into a tragedy and to
qualify this criticism as an opposition to those who 'follow the
way of the cross', neither is there any obvious reason to conjure
up the idea of a highly-organised conspiracy, other than the one
already mentioned.

The critics of the WCC form a very mixed crowd. In the
Netherlands Reformed Church, one of the founding members of the
WCC, there has always been a segment, increasing rather rapidly
at present, which is very critical of the ecumenical movement.
There are also many critical voices in the Russian Orthodox
Church, but for them it is difficult to make themselves heard
other than by way of Samizdat publications and through appeals
and letters to the outside world. In the Russian Churches the
ecumene is the official business of high churchauthorities, who
have permission to travel abroad and visit international
conferences. It is the terrain of the Department for Foreign

Relations. The rank and file of the believers have never been able to share in the ecumenical process at the parish level.

"The believers of the Russian Church never harboured any special illusions about the membership of the Moscow Patriarchate in the WCC; that act was sanctioned by the government during the period of extremely brutal persecution of religion, and obviously followed the government's own strategic aims."

wrote Gleb Yakunin and Lev Regelson to the Nairobi Assembly. The believers are cut off from information about the WCC, they do not know anything of its history, traditions and life and they belong to a church which even at the 1948 Moscow Congress appealed to all Orthodox churches to adopt the most effective measures for the purpose of preserving the principles of true Christianity in the world from the powerful seductive influence of the modern ecumenical movement. These believers sometimes realize that their leaders are not in a position to bring their sorrows and concerns before a forum of the worldchurch. Sometimes they hope that nevertheless this will be done, but they can see no signs of solidarity from the Western churches.
It is true that the West cannot be of much help in easing their situation. We know all the reasons why, but the fact remains that they have every reason to feel abandonned by fellow-Christians in the world. Is it not understandable that a certain bitterness prevails when they speak of the world ecumene? In the face of these critics we can only bow our heads.

What does it mean when the happy people in Vancouver, being able to experience the joyful and interesting gathering of the world-church, open for all their sorrows, protests and good intentions, speak about 'the link between costliness and discipleness', when some people dare to criticise some aspects of their work or doubt the relevance of it? Russian Christians, members of churches who have experienced and in many ways are still experiencing martyrdom, know better than anybody the cost of discipleship. Was there no Briton who could have reminded the Assembly of Cromwell's words: "By Christ, remember that you may be mistaken" (13) or an Orthodox churchman in the hesychast tradition who for once could have prayed aloud: Jesus Christ, Son of God, have mercy upon us, poor sinners?

Those in the Soviet Union who express views differing from the official ideology are immediately denounced as enemies of the people. This enemy-syndrome should not become characteristic for the WCC and it should show more subtilty in dealing with its critics.

Liberty and liberation

The WCC has repeatedly been criticized for its lack of solidarity with the cause of dissenting and for that reason persecuted Christians in Eastern Europe. This reproach, however, should not be directed to the Genevan office, but in the first place to the Western memberchurches themselves, who have not insisted that this should be a matter of urgent concern. It is true that the WCC is too easily inclined to tune in to the melody set by a number of influential Eastern European representatives when they interpret officially their position. But who prevents the representatives of other churches to counterbalance this and clearly state their point of view? There is of course this constant appeal to their brotherly feelings and in the corridors of the conferences they are requested not to worsen the situation which already is so difficult, by openly speaking about it and thus eventually to bring the government to prohibit further participation. Is this a sound argument? Maybe, but would it then not be better to give the collaboration with these churches a different character and restrict it to the theological, confessional dialogue and to 'the formulation of general Christian aims and principles' (one of the tasks of the CCIA?)

A growing uneasiness can be noticed in the Western churches about the silence of the WCC on human rights problems and especially the religious liberty issue in Eastern Europe. But the critique should be adressed in the first place to responsible bodies in these churches themselves and to their ecumenical representatives. The WCC should not be turned into the scapegoat of the failures of the Western churches to formulate a clear policy in respect of their ecumenical relations with Eastern European churches. When the WCC is dealing more with problems of liberation that with problems of liberty, this is also a reflection of what is happening in the churches themselves.

In the Western churches and in the small groups of those who deal with ecumenical questions, there exists a tension between those who are engaged in Third World problems and put the main emphasis on liberation, and those who occupy themselves with the Second World and give special attention to liberty. Interest in, knowledge of and contacts with the Third World are very extensive within the Western churches. This is historically understandable on the basis of the fact that the Third World is the traditional mission-field. Personal involvement in Third World problems is rather intensive especially among world-oriented, idealistic Christians. It is possible for them to go and live there and to demonstrate their solidarity with the needs and expectations of the people and to cooperate in the building up of a new society.

All this is not possible in the case of Eastern Europe. The historical ties of the churches with Eastern Europe have been few and what interest there is, is of recent date. Eastern Europe is a closed society, where young intellectuals cannot go to study social problems or engage in interesting initiatives and where the language-barrier is high. Idealistic expectations about a new future are hardly to be found there, especially after the 'Prague Spring' of 1968. On the contrary, those who really get to know that part of the world are inclined to become more and more sceptical about the ways of Marxist-Leninist socialism. During a short period the GDR has functioned as model of a new society for some groups of Christians for Socialism, but that has passed rather quickly.

There are a considerable number of reasons and acceptable explanations for the fact that the attention of those involved in ecumenical programmes of the churches has focussed on the Third World. It is regrettable however that this been accompanied by a growing neglect of the problems of the Second World and an alienation from those who occupy themselves mainly with this area. This alienation has been aggravated by the fact that involvement with Third World problems is often coupled with expectations of radical renewal which could be brought about by revolutionaty changes inspired by Marxist concepts and with a criticism of Western society which is accused of opposing this process of renewal and made responsible for the present situation.

Those who direct their attention to the Second World tend on the contrary to become more and more negative about 'the really existing socialism' and can regard only with sorrow the way in which this is sometimes presented as a new and better way of life and as a workable alternative. This is undoubtedly one of the roots of the present tensions between ecumenically oriented Christians. Those who deal with liberation dominate the ecumenical field whilst the others remain standing in front of the gate.

However, the tide is turning and a number of organisations have taken up a task which in their jugdment has been neglected by the churches and by the WCC. There is both wheat and chaff among them, but the more serious ones present to the ecumene its unpaid bills. They should not be denounced as part of an anti-ecumenical plot but taken seriously.
They should more especially be considered as an incentive for the Western member-churches to reconsider their ecumenical policy and their passive role in the collaboration with Eastern European churches. Of course, the Western churches should not dominate the WCC or use their financial or intellectual influence to dictate the agenda. This is repeated over and over again and has been understood. But an overreaction leading to isolation and 'flagellantism' is equally undesirable. The Western churches have to make up their minds and when this has been done they should

make it clear what they regard as the right policy and stand by it. The Unesco is falling to pieces mainly because the Western representatives have let things go and not earnestly tried to change the patterns when it was still possible. This should not happen to the WCC.

When the churches do not wish to restrict the agenda of the WCC to theological questions and a common counselling on general aims and purposes, but wish to engage together with the churches from communist countries in 'immediate and concrete issues' (one of the tasks of the CCIA) because they think that this is possible, then we may assume that we can deal with each other as equals. Then we may assume that we speak as brothers and not as political opponents, as free Christians and not as hostages of our political systems. In that case it must be possible to say to our Eastern European partners: if you cannot speak with us about your problems of liberty, we cannot speak with you about our problems of liberation. If you have constantly to take account in the ecumenical discussion of the possible reactions of your government, we have to take account of the possible reactions of the majority of our churchpeople.

It is not unthinkable that the pressure on the governing bodies of the Western churches may increase to such an extent that they might feel obliged to give to their participation in certain aspects of the work of the WCC a low profile. It is rather alarming that the Western participants in international bodies seem to be more inclined to retire than those from the socialist world. And the participation of the churches from Eastern Europe in the WCC is rather advantageous for their governments. It enables them to present an image of respectability and of religious freedom to the Third World, to prevent critical observations about their social and international policy and to get via the churches a trustworthy opening to public opinion in the West and the Third World. And for all this they need no concessions. The free import of Christian literature is still not allowed, except in some rare cases; any Western influence on the church membership can be prevented; information about those aspects of the ecumenical programme which are not quite acceptable can be censored; and the authorities can deal with dissenting priests, even those like Gleb Yakunin, well-known in the West, as they like. The Western churches were satisfied that he was given a bible in his prison on the eve of the Vancouver Assembly!

It seems very unlikely that the churches from the Soviet Union would be prevented by their government from continuing their participation and the same applies to the other Eastern European countries. The Western churches should not allow themselves to be silenced by threats of retreat from the churches in socialism. In determining their policy, they must among other things ask whether the CCIA is still a useful and relevant ecumenical commission and in what way it serves the ecumenical collaboration of the churches. Most Western churches have institutes and advisers at their disposal. They have well-informed commissions for Third World problems, a great deal of expertise and a network of relations with these churches. Most of these bilateral and multilateral ecumenical contacts pass beyond the CCIA. It has become quite clear that statements on international affairs, which have been drawn up together with representatives from communist countries do not carry much weight and have repeatedly caused much trouble. The communist governments disregard them completely, as for that matter do Western governments. But what is more serious is that the Western public opinion has begun to have doubts and as public opinion is the only means for the churches to influence governments' policies these statements are losing their relevance and have an opposite effect to what they were really intended to achieve.

Bishop W. Krusche has said that the churches must act independently in their own context, and the truth of this again became evident at the Vancouver Assembly. A resolution on the policy of the USA in Central America and one on Afghanistan were proposed by the CCIA. The fact that these two resolutions were proposed is a reminder of what has been called 'the central conviction' of the WCC, that there should be no selectivity in its prophetic witness. But the very different tone of the two resolutions caused fierce controversies and gave rise to very negative reactions, not because of a dark conspiracy of hostile forces, but because of the failure of the WCC 'to speak with one voice' as a GDR representative remarked. What could have happened if the WCC had had to operate without a CCIA?

The resolution on Central-America was a clear expression of what the National Council of Churches in the USA thinks and has stated before about this aspect of the policy of its government. The American churches could have told the Assembly: we have adopted a resolution on Latin America. We are going to present this resolution to our government. We will discuss it with you here and take note of your remarks, but it is our resolution about the policy of our government. We invite you to discuss with us what you have done in your country.
That would have been very stimulating even if no resolution on Afghanistan had been proposed by the Russian churches. To challenge the churches in communist countries to explain why they cannot speak and act as the churches in Western democracies, cannot possibly be considered as unbrotherly. Let us exchange ideas about the task of the church in society, but not at all costs try to pass together resolutions adressed to governments on matters of immediate concern. For the orthodox it might even be a

blessing if they are freed from the obligation to participate in all these Western horizontal activities!

The Western churches try to fulfill their critical function in society, maybe not everywhere and always, but the CCIA does not contribute much to it. One of its aims is 'to encourage respect for and observance of human rights and fundamental freedoms, special attention being given to the problem of religious liberty'; another aim is: 'to suggest ways in which Christians may act effectively upon these problems in their respective countries and internationally.' But unfortunately little help has come from the CCIA in defining a policy for the churches on religious liberty in Eastern Europe, given that the WCC itself cannot do much in this field. How can we support our sisterchurches living in Marxism-Leninism, which are estranged from their task of witnessing and serving in society and subjected to a neo-constantinian enslavement which wants to change them into a collective chorus of assent, a temporary decoration on the facade of socialism and a cultic ghetto?

What has the CCIA done to stimulate the information and research done in the churches on Eastern Europe? The section of the Vancouver report devoted to World Affairs in Ecumenical Perspective (14) says:

"It is imperative that member churches and the WCC continue to identify and denounce gross violations of religious freedom and extend moral and material assistance to those who suffer oppression and even persecution because of their religious beliefs and practices."

This is a very courageous statement, but did the representatives realize what the consequences would be? Experience has shown that the WCC can do and does do very little for the implementation of the fundamental right of social relgous liberty in Eastern Europe. If this is not openly recognized the disappointment and the criticism will increase. Would it not have been wiser to admonish the memberchurches to be more diligent in this matter and to formulate their own policy how to deal with this issue?

The Western member-churches should take common counsel -as do the memberchurches in Eastern Europe- on how they can act together in international affairs, especially in the field of human rights. One of the fundamental questions should then be: do the memberchurches really still accept the fundamental aim of the CCIA 'witness to the lordship of Christ over man and history by serving mankind in the field of international relations?' It seems that a rather influential group of churches for confessional and socio-political reasons does not really accept

this anymore or interprets it in a way which is not in accordance
with its original meaning.

Western churches have their specific responsibilities

At a meeting of young and dedicated activists of Amnesty
International a Russian historian, lately emigrated or rather
expelled from his country, reported his experiences in prison and
psychiatric clinics in the Soviet Union. As a member of a human
rights group he was imprisoned for three and a half years, but
according to his testimony he had been treated better than most
of his co-prisoners because of the fact that his case had become
known in the West and numerous letters had been sent to make it
clear that his case had not remained unnoticed in the rest of the
world.

The work of Amnesty International, and other organisations
like the International Commission of Jurists, has gained
recognition and popularity in church circles, but not because it
conforms to the prejudices of Western church people. These
organisations earnestly try not to be selective in their
protection of those persecuted for conscience's sake. They
endeavour to put into practice what the Vancouver Assembly called
upon the churches to do: to identify and denounce gross
violations of religious freedom and extend moral and material
assistance to those who suffer oppression and even persecution
because of their beliefs and practices. Neither do they usually
do this 'from a safe distance, i.e. from outside the country in
question' as the already quoted CCIA pamphlet suggests. Only in
those cases where their activities are expressly forbidden by the
governments are they forced to speak from outside the country,
although their evidence is always based on testimonies from those
directly concerned.
We know of course that these organisations have a different
methodology from that of the WCC. They are orientated towards
action and deal directly with individual cases of human rights
violations, more especially in the field of civic and political
rights. This is a restricted task, but worthy and honest and it
should be accomplished.

The WCC has set itself a much wider task. In the Vancouver
statement on Human Rights (15) we read:

"The Nairobi Assembly affirmed its commitment to the
promotion of human rights under the following categories: the
right to basic quarantees of life; the rights to
self-determination, to cultural identity and the rights of
minorities; the right to participate in decision-making
within the community; the right to dissent; the right to
personal dignity; and the right to religious freedom.

Following Nairobi, the churches have seen the need to broaden their understanding of human rights to include the right to peace, the right to protection of the environment, the right to development and the right to know one's rights and to struggle for them."

The churches regard it as their mission to be a church-for-others and to commit themselves to the care for and the protection of human life in all its individual and social dimensions. An immense and never-ending task. Nobody can possibly survey the whole field but it is a good advice not to absolutize one aspect at the cost of others. The whole issue of human rights cannot be restricted to religious liberty in Marxist states and the broadening of the human rights concept is beneficial but it should not function as an excuse for leaving certain aspects aside or rendering suspect those who deal especially with one aspect.

The image of a clinic presents itself, where specialists for all the human diseases are working. The ophtalmologist knows that there are more parts of the human body than the eye and so do the dentist and the psychiatrist. They also know that the different parts belong together and influence each other. But still, they are dealing with their own specialism. Thus it is with the many aspects of human rights. Nobody should deny that there are other aspects than those which he is dealing with, but everybody has his specific task.

A contribution of the Commission on Public Affairs of the Evangelical Church in Germany, "Human Rights in the Ecumenical Discussion", presented to the Nairobi Assembly, says:

"The Western understanding of Human Rights is oriented towards the individual person's right to life. Human Rights are intended to achieve and guarantee the worth of his/her existence as a human being (...) This Western understanding of Human Rights is at present confronted by two other conceptions of Human Rights which are formed along more collective lines:
  a. According to Marxism-Leninism, Human Rights in socialist societies are secured automatically. In this view, Human Rights are identical with the right and the obligation to participate in the realization of socialism as defined by this doctrine. In theory, therefore, no conflict can exist between Human Rights and the legal structure of these countries.
  b. Wherever there is a struggle for Human Rights in African, Asian or South American countries, by and large it is not a matter of the recognition and promotion of individual interests; rather, the struggle is usually on behalf of

the freedom, self-determination and right to live of peoples and nations.

Christians must try to understand, value and respect the different viewpoints on Human Rights as the expression of different political and social situations and problems. However, they must never content themselves with the fact that today practically all political systems make verbal professions of Human Rights.

It is much more important,

- to determine existing areas of agreement, and, so far as possible, to make them the basis of speaking and acting together in the world,
- to recognize clearly and express the differences in interpretations, and
- to explain and communicate to advocates of other conceptions of Human Rights the historical experience which has led to the distinctly Western version of Human Rights. In particular, the experience must be communicated that worthwhile human existence cannot be guaranteed without the protection of the individual from the despotism and destruction caused by the state."

Of outstanding importance in this passage is the underlining of the specific responsibility of the churches in the West to work for the implementation of those aspects of human rights which tend to be forgotten or neglected by others.

The WCC has repeatedly admonished the churches not to neglect their task and not to expect too much from the WCC. Some churches are doing their homework rather well. The United Presbyterians in the USA, for instance, publish at regular intervals surveys of religious liberty throughout the world on the basis of stated criteria and draw up a list of the most repressive states. It would not be possible for the World Council, which includes churches not allowed to conduct a critical survey of the situation in their homeland, to adopt such a 'denunciatory approach', but it is not forbidden for member-churches to use this method. Neither should member-churches feel ashamed when they emphasise the rights of individual freedom and plead for their implementation. A certain imbalance, to the detriment of religious liberty, can sometimes be found in WCC publications and they appear to suggest that we have moved on from the former emphasis on religious liberty to more important social concerns.

"Concentration has shifted away from a more partial approach to human rights where religious freedom was sometimes given exclusive or exceptional attention."

wrote the CCIA in its report to the Nairobi Assembly (16). This was repeated in 1982 (17):

""Human Rights are fundamentally a struggle for liberation of an entire community. The earlier WCC emphasis on religious liberty provided a point of departure for a more integral approach to human rights."

An integral approach is praiseworthy, but it does not mean that the advocacy of the implementation of religious liberty is no longer a part of this integral approach and belongs to the past history of the ecumenical movement. "The right to religious freedom has been and continues to be a major concern of member-churches and the WCC" says the Nairobi report on Human Rights (18). But the next sentence immediately contains a critical warning: "However this right should never be seen as belonging exclusively to the Church." As if this has ever been propagated by the ecumenical movement.

The old doctrine of liberty only for the 'recta conscientia', the conscience which is in accordance with objective truth, was defended by some very conservative members of the Second Vatican Council in the beginning of the discussion on religious liberty, but they were quickly told that the Church's conception of religious liberty has completely changed. The official ideologists of the communist party still accept this doctrine but one never hears a church, which is a member of the WCC, defend it.

It is good that the Nairobi-report draws our attention to the fact that churches should not only plead for their own religious liberty without active respect for the faith and rights of others. The churches have certainly done too little for the persecuted Marxists in Czechoslovakia after 1968 and do not sufficiently realize that in Marxist countries Christians are not the only victims of restrictions. But it is not certain that this was what was meant by the Nairobi-report.

There is a tendency in publications on religious liberty, issuing from the WCC, to discourage those who are dealing with the situation under Marxist-Leninism. The study-paper on Religious Liberty, submitted for information by the CCIA in 1980, has not been accepted by the member-churches. No reactions were sent in by them and so the study has not been pursued.

It is regrettable that this report, which is rather representative of the way in which the CCIA is presently dealing with religious liberty, has not been overtly rejected. The churches should take papers sent to them by the WCC more seriously and if these are not acceptable not just file them among the irrelevant mail (19). One passage can serve as an illustration how those who deal with the situation in Marxist countries are discouraged:

"The issue of religious liberty itself should not be used or misused for political ends. The increasing use by governments of the religious liberty issue as a propaganda weapon against other states has led to an increasing politization of understanding and discussion of this issue."

Is it true that the human rights issue was only inserted by the West in the Helsinki-agreement to focus attention on the misdeeds of others and to draw the attention of the public to human rights violations in Eastern Europe? Are those who ask for the implementation of the rights of religious liberty misusing the issue for political ends and as a propaganda weapon against the offending state? William van den Bercken (20) points out that: "The politics of the Soviet Union evoke in progressive circles in the West only so-called secondary reactions, i.e. actions against reactions." Is this what the report is doing?

It is said that more attention is being paid to the deficiencies of other nations than to critical self-examination.
"Those who live within any given location are best qualified to interpret and analyse their own experience and are best able to prescribe strategies for the realization of human rights within their own situation."

stated the CCIA in a report to the 1979 meeting of the WCC Central Committee in Jamaica. Does this mean that we must ignore the situation in Marxist countries and that we must not 'see the problems of others through the lenses of our own histories, theologies and world-views." as the CCIA-report Uppsala to Nairobi remarked. "Religious liberty", continues the report, "remains a priority concern, but is now seen in the context of other recognized rights and worked at much more in terms of the particular historical situation in which it is endangered." But what does all this really mean? Can we no longer in speaking about the situation in a communist country use 'the lens' of a Christian conviction as summarized in the Nairobi statement on Human Rights:

"By religious freedom we mean the freedom to have or to adopt a religion or belief of one's choice, and freedom, either individually or in community with others and in public or private, to manifest one's religion or belief in worship, observance, practice and teaching. Religious freedom should also include the right and duty of religious bodies to criticize the ruling powers when necessary, on the basis of their religious convictions." "A yardstick of christian responsibility" (O.F. Nolde) has been given in the many international churchdeclarations, but now we are admonished to work for religious liberty in terms of particular historical situations for instance in the Soviet Union. A

Professor at the Moscow University Law Faculty (21) described the Marxist conception of freedom only for the 'recta conscientia' as follows:

"Genuine freedom of opinion is not any unhindered dissemination of ideas, judgments, etc., but only the free dissemination of progressive and revolutionary views, ideas and opinions, which correspond to the interests of the popular masses – the carriers of social progress, the moving force of history. Only under this condition is it possible to talk about genuine freedom of opinion, in particular about freedom of speech, of the press, of assembly, etc. Marxism-Leninism rejects a formal approach to this problem. Only the free and unhindered dissemination of such ideas, views and jugdments, which further social progress and correspond to the interests of the broad popular masses and to their enlightment and spiritual enrichment, may be regarded as genuine freedom of speech, of the press, of assembly, and, generally of opinion."

The Vancouver Statement says:
"Cooperation in the field of human rights is emerging between the Christian community and people of other living faiths and ideologies, based on their common commitment to human values and social goals."

As far as Marxism is concerned this is a rather euphemistic statement. The Marxist and Christian conceptions of religious liberty are so different that before we can cooperate in this field, some serious discussions are necessary. It is regrettable that these have not yet come about and that the WCC neither invites the Marxist ideologists to such a discussion, nor starts a study without them. For how can we work otherwise at the problem of religious liberty in terms of the particular situation in the Soviet Union? And how can we assume that the Christians in the Soviet Union are best able to prescribe strategies for the realization of human rights in their situation? They cannot even acknowledge that there are any problems!

Western churches must either take the initiative to start a discussion on the fundamental principle of religious liberty in Marxist-Leninist countries and about the actual situation there or take more seriously the work already being done in this field. Western churches will have to denounce the gross violations of religious liberty and extend moral and material assistance to those who suffer oppression and even persecution because of their religious beliefs and practices. They should not pretend that they have to wait for official complaints from their sister churches' leadership because these will not be forthcoming. But the church is more than bishops and synods. Numerous complaints do reach the West from church members and, without indulging in theories about the true and false church, current in some circles, one can hear the voice of the church in many samizdat publications and in letters which are sent, even if they do not bear the seal of a synod.

The Western churches should take very seriously what is said in WCC studies and declarations about the many dimensions of human rights and the integral approach of their implementation. But they should reject all those casual remarks which seem to throw doubt upon the good intentions of those who deal with religious liberty problems in Eastern Europe, and which tend to suggest that no problems exist in Marxist countries, neither in the sphere of legislation nor in the sphere of practical application. They should strongly resist any pressure to strike religious liberty from the agenda, and must not allow it to disappear quietly under the table. Some churches could covenant together to deal more specifically with this issue. There are churches which have a tradition in this field and which command expert knowledge. There should, however, be a close collaboration and a more serious discussion about a common strategy than the existing human rights commissions of the CCIA, which have a very low profile (22) can provide. All this should not be done in an antagonistic spirit - in the ecumenical movement we do not behave as 'hostile' churches - but with respect for the churches concerned and with the intention of helping them in their mission without, however, forgetting about those who suffer oppression and even persecution because of their religious beliefs and practices.
What we need now is a strategy which will help the ecumenical movement to extend assistance to them.

A strategy of assistance

The dilemma is often presented as: either silent diplomacy or public protest. But it might well be that this is a false antithesis and that these two methods belong intrinsically together.

The then General-Secretary of the WCC said in an interview (23): "Our faith is a scandal, it's an offence. And if we are to carry out our mission in the world, we become an offence to the world. Jesus did not promise us anything more than the hatred of the world."
But as soon as the question of liberty rights and ideological oppression in the Soviet Union comes into the picture we usually hear very different tones. Then one gets the impression that there are two world councils: the one courageous, challenging even audacious, counting all things to be loss, defying the

mighty; the other prudent, diplomatic, fawning in the presence of the mighty, shunning all offence.

There is of course room for silent diplomatic actions, but this ought to be part of a broader strategy. It is very difficult to pass judgement on the content and scope of silent diplomacy, because its most conspicious feature is its secrecy, but one might ask what the results are. It is often the case that when unexpected concessions are made, organisations claim it as the result of their prudent and diplomatic procedures. The contrary cannot usually be proved. One may suppose by way of example that permission to import a bible commentary in Russian, translated and printed in the West, for the Evangelical Christian Baptists is the result of the diplomatic contacts of the Baptist World Alliance with the State Council for Religious Affairs; and the same applies to the permission given for importing a large number of new hymnbooks for the Brethren Church in Czechoslovakia in 1979.

However, many contacts with state authorities scarcely seem to bear any fruit. The first official visit of a representative of the Soviet State Council for Religious Affairs to the World Council in Geneva in December 1984 (24), apparently passed without any concessions on the part of this council. One might have hoped that this visit would be preceded by the release of Gleb Yakunin, sentenced in 1980 to five years in a strict regime labor camp, to be followed by five years of internal exile. He was one of the inaugurators of the Christian Committee for the Defense of Believers' Rights in the USSR. Yakunin's memorandum to the Nairobi Assembly did play a role in his trial and the WCC addressed itself in October 1980 to the Russian Orthodox Church to convey the concern of the ecumenical fellowship. Metropolitan Yuvenaly sent an answer conceding that the WCC does have the right to pose questions about it.

This was all according to the newly-established pattern of consultation of the churches concerned and the letters were even published. The Russian Orthodox Church did what it could, but this unfortunately is very little. A remark in Yuvenaly's letters about a misuse of the issue of religious freedom for cold war-propaganda indicates that the State Council undoubtedly had a hand in the drafting of the letter. Yuvenaly writes:
"Unfortunately many aspects of the life of our society, inlcuding human rights and questions of religious freedom in particular, are often reflected by Western information agencies in an extremely distorted manner, in the spirit of so-called psychological warfare. No small wonder, then, that as a rule, a distorted perspective of these questions is created abroad." (25)

It is regrettable that even when the WCC expresses the concern in the churches about a case like this the cold war accusation comes up. The letter of Konrad Raiser, Acting General Secretary, on the contrary underlinded the constant endeavours of the WCC to establish 'an atmosphere conductive to détente' and the fact that 'a series of trials such as those in process now can only make that task immensely more difficult'. It is the trials and not the Western reactions which are conductive to a cold war atmosphere.

The Russian Orthodox Church is absolutely powerless in a case like this. Metropolitan Filaret said in a London interview (26): ""The path followed by Father Yakunin cannot be the way of our church and its hierarchy. We do not intend to enter into conflict with the authorities. In a situation like ours, our duty is to preach the Gospel and to extend pastoral aid to our flock."

But after the exchange of letters nothing has happened and we do not know whether the matter was raised again in the correspondence which undoubtedly preceded the visit of Pyotr V. Makartsev, vice-chairman of the Council for Religious Affairs, who had come to Geneva 'to answer questions about the church in the USSR today'.

Do we really help the churches in communist countries by frequent contacts with the state secretariats? After every visit to or meeting with ecumenical representatives in Eastern Europe we read that visitors were received by the representatives of the State Council for Religious Affairs. On these occasions the officials show a paternalistic care for 'their' churches which have guests from abroad. But are we not, by these frequent courtesy visits, accepting and acknowledging the rights which these state authorities presume to have over 'their' churches? Are they not a silent recognition of a very reprehensible predominance of the state over the church? Should Western church representatives not show more reluctance in accepting this sort of formality and resist the temptation of being treated as 'important' visitors?

One of the most revealing news items concerning the visit of a state secretary for church affairs to the West can be found in the press-service of the Hungarian Ecumenical Council (27), where the visit is reported of the Hungarian state-secretary, I. Miklos, to the Ministry of Cults of the government of North-Rhine Westphalen (BRD). Miklos came, accompanied by the reformed bishop K. Toth as his advisor, to discuss the relations between the protestant churches of both countries and how the churches could contribute to peace and détente in Europe. A curious mission for an official of a communist state, where the illusion of a complete separation of church and state is carefully maintained.

It would be advisable for a set of guidelines to be worked out by the churches for the use of visitors in Eastern Europe. Rome has a school for church diplomats, but the Western member churches of the WCC definitely have not and quite a few blunders have been made.

These guidelines could include the suggestion never to make a public statement before departure from the country. Such statements or convenient passages from then have too often been misused for propagandistic purposes. Another recommendation might be never to accept an invitation for a meeting in an Eastern European country sponsored by the government of that country (for instance a peace-congress) or to receive a government official without demanding some small concessions which could be helpful for the churches. It would not be difficult to enumerate a number of points which could be raised. Why not for instance demand the release of Yakunin before receiving a high Soviet official - this could easily be accorded and is not asking for the impossible,
Another point is that no group of church visitors should ever allow the government of the guest country to decide its composition by allowing entry to some and refusing it to others. It is equally important that every visitor should try to break through the wall which is shutting him off from contacts with ordinary believers. Visits are arranged in such a way that usually one meets only those who are allowed to have contacts with foreigners. The importance of contacts and meetings should not be exaggerated, but they can be useful for the life of the church if the visitors succeed in conveying the solidarity of the Western churches with their host-churches and their concern with those who suffer because of the confinements to which they are subjected.

The ecumenical movement has always stressed the need for personal contacts. O.F. Nolde (28) summed up some 'clear-cut requirements' from ecumenical statements, as for instance:

""Commitment to make and use opportunities for personal contacts between people in opposing countries as a means of easing tensions and promoting better understanding. Keep alive the sense of fellowship with all people separated by articifical curtains and seek continuously a sympathetic understanding of changing conditions so that opportunities for personal contacts may be effectively used whenever and wherever they appear." But another requirement is: "Recognize the danger of totalitarianism which seeks to capture the souls of men and to control the life of communities - in whatever form or in whatever land it may appear - and devise methods of resistance which under existing circumstances may prove most effective."

Another former WCC officer, Albert van den Heuvel, said during the Nairobi debate on religious liberty (29):

"I learned that we cannot speak about human rights in Eastern Europe... if we do not put it in the context of fraternal relationships and if we do not devise a language of respect and sympathy for all those churches who witness in another social system."

But at the same time he acknowledged that churches dare not be silent.

The Nairobi report which resulted from the discussion stated:

"The solidarity which results from faith in our common Lord permits the mutual sharing of joys and sufferings and requires mutual correction. Christians dare not remain silent when other members of the Body of Christ face problems in any part of the world. But whatever is said and done must be preceded by consultation and must be an expression of Christian love."

Basic criteria for any action in the defense of human rights should be:

"to cultivate the spirit of reconciliation in order to make possible better relations between conflicting powers... and to have an objective point of view which will avoid hysterics or hatred"; to assist the churches and the Christians in their plight and to show solidarity and 'sympathetic identification with those suffering from the curtailment or denial of human rights" (Nolde)

Consultation with the churches concerned should be part of any action, but we should always bear in mind their extremely limited possibilities and the pressure exerted on them to do everything they can to suppress any action in the sphere of human rights and religious liberty. We should not allow ourselves to be drawn into the captivity in which these churches have to live. Silent diplomacy is equally part of a strategy of assistance. The authorities should know about the concern in the rest of the world for those who are suffering and be given the chance to redress injustice, show mercy or make concessions without losing face. But it is a way full of pitfalls. Contacts between church and state in Eastern Europe are always taking place in complete secrecy and church people have become very suspicious about them. In the synod of the Churchprovince Saxony (GDR) in October 1976, the problem of the continuous negotiations between the church leadership and the authorities – necessary because the constitution does not clearly define the freedoms of the church – was openly discussed. It was asked: do these contacts not alienate the church leaders from the pastors and are they not inclined in view of the next round of talks, in which they might want to obtain certain concessions, to avoid bringing up points which are controversial and which could endanger other aspects of the work of the church? The church people, however, expect a witness by their leaders that does them justice.

This also applies to the secret diplomacy of our Western church leaders in their contact with communist governments. The whole issue should be openly talked over, not only in a GDR synod, but in WCC meetings and Western synods.

Actions outside the sphere of publicity can be effective only if the communist authorities are fully convinced that other forms of actions are equally possible. Nolde said: "Greater reliance must be placed upon public opinion - both domestic and worldwide as a means of assuring that governments honor their commitments." This must be an integral part of a strategy of assistance. The churches have to be consistent and neither sacrifice their witness on the altar of unity nor their advocacy for the oppressed on the altar of confessional conversations. Nor must they shrink from their obligations in the face of cold war accusations which inevitably follow any public action. Individuals who are victimized by unjust laws must be sure that they are not forgotten by the ecumenical fellowship. A strategy must be worked out by the churches and suitable methods devised for denouncing gross violations of religious freedom and assisting those who suffer oppression and even persecution. In the case of religious liberty issues in communist countries little can be expected from the WCC because it is handicapped by the position of a number of member churches, and thus the other churches will have to act on their own responsibility. The Nairobi Assembly stated:

"The churches will also be concerned with those clauses in the Helsinki Agreement which deal directly with their own position and functions (religious freedom, freedom of belief and worship, contacts between the churches, exchange of information etc). They will make clear to the governments their own understanding of these sections and how they could be implemented."

It also declared: "We are called to be the voice of the voiceless and the advocates of the oppressed." In respect to the situation in Eastern Europe little has been done by the churches and the CCIA has not given much encouragement. The initiative taken at Nairobi has petered out and has not been taken over by the member churches. The full implementation of religious liberty should remain (or once more become) a concern for all ecumenical Christians and churches.

NOTES

1. What in the world is the World Council of Churches? Risk series, Geneva 1978.
2. Erich Weingärtner, Human Rights on the Ecumenical Agenda. Background Information CCIA 1983/3, p.10
3. See: A.F. Carillo de Albornoz, The basis of religious liberty, WCC 1963, p. 35, 36
4. See: Religious Liberty in the Soviet Union. WCC and USSR - a post Nairobi documentation. Edited by Michael Bourdeaux, Hans Hebly, Eugen Voss. Keston College, London 1976, pp.12, 15
5. See: A study-report on religious liberty accepted by the Central Committee Geneva 1980. Background Information CCIA, 1981-4; and the publication by Erich Weingärtner mentioned in note 2
6. See the essay: The post-war ecumenical dream in Europe
7. Background Information CCIA, 1981-4
8. Nairobi to Vancouver 1975-1983. Report of the Central Committee to the Sixth Assembly of the WCC, Geneva 1983, p.157
9. Gathered for Life. Official Report VI Assembly WCC, Geneva 1983, p. 117-5-1
10. Crypts of Power, London 1971, pp.198, 193
11. Isaac Rottenberg in: Christianity Today, 20 March 1983
12. Gathered for Life, p. 185
13. Quoted by Max Kohnstamm. Ecumenical Review, Vol 37, nr. 1, Jan. 1985, p.119
14. Gathered for Life, p. 142
15. Gathered for Life, p. 138-144
16. Uppsala to Nairobi. Geneva 1975, p. 135
17. Acting in faith. Geneva 1982, p. 40
18. Breaking Barriers. Nairobi 1975, p. 106
19. See for critical evaluation: J.A. Hebly, Religionsfreiheit und der O.R.K., Ökumenische Rundschau, 32. Jhrg., Jan. 1983
20. Internationale Spectator, December 1981, p. 758
21. Quoted: The Russians and the WCC, p. 136
22. Nairobi to Vancouver, p. 138
23. What in the World is the World Council of Churches, p. 4
24. Ecumenical Press Service 85-01-18.; One World no. 102, 1985 p. 60, 61
25. Ecumenical Press Service nr. 30, 13 Nov. 1980
26. January 1980. See: Istina 1981, p. 421
27. U.K.P. 15 October 1983
28. The Churches and the Nations, p. 175
29. Breaking Barriers, p. 170, 174

INDEX OF PERSONS

Name

Dr. J.A. (Hans) Hebly (1923) received his doctorate in theology
from Utrecht University. From 1949 to 1951 he was an ecumenical
fieldworker in the Cimade (Paris); from 1951 to 1970 he served as
a minister in the Netherlands Reformed Church. Since 1970 he has
been staff-member of the Interacademical Institute for
Missiological and Ecumenical Research, Utrecht, the Netherlands,
of which at present he is the director. He has been closely
involved in the ecumenical movement and is one of the founding
members of Societas Oecumenica, the European Society for
Ecumenical Research. He is the author, apart from numerous
articles, of: Proselitism as an Ecumenical Problem (1962, in
Dutch); Protestants in Russia (1973); Churches in Eastern Europe
(1975, in Dutch); The Russians and the World Council of Churches
(1978); Church in Socialism (1979, in Dutch, about the GDR); The
Struggle for Peace (1983, in Dutch), and the New Confession of
Faith of the Evangelical Christian Baptists (1983, in Dutch).